HOUSES

ALSO BY MARIETTE HIMES GOMEZ

Rooms

HOUSES

INSIDE AND OUT

MARIETTE HIMES GOMEZ

COLLINS | DESIGN

An Imprint of HarperCollinsPublishers

    HarperCollins books may be purchased for educational,
business, or sales promotional use. For information please write:
Special Markets Department, HarperCollins Publishers,
10 East 53rd Street, New York, NY 10022.

FIRST EDITION

Designed by Joel Avirom, Jason Snyder and Meghan Day Healey

Library of Congress Cataloging-in-Publication Data has been
applied for.

ISBN 13: 978-0-06-112422-8
ISBN 10: 0-06-112422-2

07 08 09 10 11 */ TOP 10 9 8 7 6 5 4 3 2 1

I lovingly dedicate this book to

Brooke and Alexander Gomez.

We have shared our lives and houses

in Shelter Island, Long Island,

and New York City.

CONTENTS

PROLOGUE

TO THE READER

A house is an idea, a house is a thing, a house is you, a tangible embodiment of your dreams and desires and interests. Your house has its own personality and continuity and unity. Its parts come together as your home. My conviction that houses are wholes that express the spirit of the inhabitants forms the core of this book. It is the premise underlying my approach to designing a house. It is the inspiration for my reflections on houses in the text, and it is the basis for the visual presentation of the houses in pictures. In keeping with the idea that houses are more than their rooms or their planks and tiles and wallpaper, the book emphasizes both verbally and visually the integrity of the house in its entirety, and not as a jumble of scattered parts. I have kept houses together to respect this idea. I have not deconstructed them so that you would have to put them back together again like a house of cards. I have presented them to show that they have their own character, that they are themselves, so that you experience their balance and harmony and flow.

This is the cadence of the book.

You will see a whole house unfold in a chapter, although parts of it may apply to the content of another house when I illustrate concepts or individual aspects of houses. As I discuss a fireplace or object, lighting or the placement of art and mirrors, you may see and remember that fireplace from another part of the book. But houses are kept as units for understanding.

When a house is seen as a whole, not a collection of fragments thrown together, it transforms the house into a home, with spirit and harmony.

MY FIRST HOUSES

I grew up in a small Midwestern town where families ate meals together and chatted on porches. Ours was a stone house, with a big glassed-in porch and neoclassical columns. The houses of my grandmothers, my aunts, and my mother were welcoming, attractive places with loving people and good food. The emphasis was on comfort and family. The houses wrapped themselves around our lives, and they had love in them. They echoed with years of stored family life. These warm memories are with me all the time.

I remember the snowstorms and the backyards filled with flowers and my favorite trees and asparagus plants. I knew our garden by heart. An important part of childhood, especially in the Midwest, is playing outdoors. I remember the porches: the stone porch, where I had my tea parties; my grandmother's porch, where we would go

after Sunday lunch and sit and talk; and the front porch of my other grandmother, where we would sit in the early evening with her neighbors in the small town in northern Michigan. Porches gave a sense of community. They were for being with people, with neighbors and family, for togetherness. They were between inside and out, house and garden.

Kitchens, too, come to mind from those early houses. There was my grandmother's kitchen, where I would wait while she made me a snack. My mother and her sister would go into our kitchen to do the dishes after dinner, to chat and catch up. When I design kitchens today, I make sure they are spaces that encourage families to gather, as we did then. There

were always comfortable chairs in those houses. There were windows that allowed the sunlight to stream in, and there was a piano in every house.

As I grew up in that small Michigan town, I became aware that there was more than one kind of house. My friend's house was laid out differently. The features of the houses affected me. Even as a child, I was conscious of where I was sitting or the lamp I liked, of the coziness of the house or the way the dining room was set up. I remember the wallpapers—some floral, some geometric. I always reacted to these things, and very early on I knew that I wanted to be a designer.

I believe that I was born with the gene for design—it was not a matter of circumstance, there was no request to decorate a friend's house, for example. Something inside me told me that I

LEFT
A former dairy farm that today provides the setting for contemporary weekend living.

ABOVE
A refurbished barn brings with it a modern level of comfort.

was going to do it, and I did. My mother and my aunts became my role models in decorating.

When I married and we bought our first house in Clinton Hill, Brooklyn, and renovated it, I did the same kinds of things my mother would have done. I made a cozy dining room, a kitchen that worked, and a living room that was interesting for friends when they came over. We had moved to Brooklyn because we thought we were going to live in a big house there with our children. But then the commute to New York necessitated a change in location. We decided we needed to be in the city again, and so we had to forgo the luxury of space and air and trees. As a solution, we bought three barns on Long Island and renovated them. They had been dairy barns, and their history became part of the experience. Planning how the rooms worked and what they would look like—to make a barn work as a living environment for a family—was a new project altogether. And it turned out to be a spectacular success. Doing the barns and the house in Brooklyn with my husband, Raymond Gomez, an architect, enhanced my love of houses, and I have learned much along the way.

It was a different time then. With more experience and education, my style now may have become more sophisticated, but I still emphasize coziness. When I approach a house, the comfort and warmth, the dinners and evenings on the porches of my childhood, are part of my awareness. It was all about those houses. The houses I live in reflect, in part, my past.

All houses tell stories of past and present. It's in the choice of chairs and in the collection of painted boxes on your coffee table, and it's in the house itself. The past gave the Long Island barns we renovated a particular originality. The past gives character and spirit to my house and yours, setting them apart from others, making them unique.

I like to recognize that all houses are repositories of history and stories and meanings. You feel that somewhere in the air there are the lives lived and living under the roof. That is how a particular house can develop a mystique—one that a room does

*This side elevation balances
out the roofline.*

not have. Think of *The House of the Seven Gables* or
Wuthering Heights. Houses reverberate with the color
and character of all of their inhabitants. I like to be
aware of this dimension, which goes beyond the
visible, even if it is not directly reflected in physical
details. It gives an aura of many-layered experience to
the life of the house, an added depth and richness
to the perceptual grasp of walls and windows.

　　To me, houses are mirrors. From childhood, I've
known that one of the most important things in life
is your house and how it reflects your personality.
Your own space will be your own space, even in an
apartment, but a house is an embellished extension of
your ego, not just a costume party. It has to have humor
and spirit and soul, and even a flourish!

　　I especially enjoy the process of turning houses
into homes. That is why I feel strongly about writing this
book about houses, because it is not about decorating
alone. I see a house as a living concept and as a lifestyle
choice. As it was in the houses of my childhood, and as
it was with the barns, it's about how the house serves
the needs of its inhabitants and how it tells your story.

　　Owning a house is also an important part of the
American dream. Ownership of ground and dwelling gives us a
sense of security, and security is paramount. I think of my house
as my personal space—and my safety net. Everything you want from
a house can be part of the choices you make. At various times your
house will also be your jumping-off point, or your cocoon to sink
into, or your own private work of art—these are all important aspects
of your house.

　　From taking shelter in caves, we have evolved and elaborated
our dwellings into houses as we know them now. We have gone
from cave paintings to wallpaper and semigloss. Cave, hut, cottage,
mansion: houses embrace us. They express us. Houses are about
us. We love them.

IN THE BEGINNING

LOVE AT FIRST SIGHT

What happens when a little voice says, "Time for your own house"? After school, college, or marriage comes the inevitable decision about where to live. Statistics indicate that home ownership is our first choice. We choose houses over apartments for their particular enticements—land, windows and natural light, privacy, several floors, outdoor living space. People are driven to acquire their own homes in order to express their individuality and to answer personal lifestyle needs. What about that charming house I dream about? Then reality hits. Can we afford to buy, move, and furnish? These are mental flashcards and the possibilities are various. We live in the city and would love to have a getaway, a country or summer place. Should we have a house that serves both purposes? Images crowd our minds.

For the exterior of this Long Island house, which has seen three generations,
blue hydrangeas lining the walkway are part of the color scheme,
to go with the soft yellow clapboard house and cedar roof.

This immaculately restored house in Ireland is tucked into a lush landscape.

ABOVE
*Gates and cobblestones at the rear
of the house give a feeling of history
to one entrance.*

RIGHT
Grounds that a park would envy.

Then suddenly you see a house, and you know it is right. This is the time to go with your instincts and grab it. You can't program or anticipate or duplicate the feeling— it's instantaneous. You know this should be your house. It is important to seize that moment, to trust love at first sight. My heart belonged to my Long Island house as soon as I drove up to it, in spite of the problems the real-estate agent warned me about. Other people can't read what comes from your soul, the instant at which a house embeds itself in your mind and your heart. Houses are personal, from that first meeting, the blind date, all the way through your decisions about future shape and design, through the personality you give it and the stories you infuse it with. This is why a house is more than roof tiles and clapboards.

Houses are combinations of practicalities and ideas, aesthetics and domesticities, work and love. When we find the right house, it draws upon all our faculties, all the parts of our lives, and our decision-making powers. It corrals the architect and the handyman, the art gallery, the tree trimmer, the children, the dog, and the birds in the tree to create the living space that frames our lives. All aspects of our dwelling deserve our attention in the creation. Your creativity and personal investment, along with the initial falling in love, will make your house distinctive and dazzling from start to finish.

FIRST THINGS FIRST

CHRONOLOGY—THE NATURAL ORDER OF HOUSES

In the beginning, time and space and chronology and geography are fundamental.

Because houses relate to the cycle of life, both individual and family, they have an inherent natural order, a chronology, that single rooms don't have. I am always mindful of the resonance of houses as spaces where this subtle and complex order of living is played out, from formal to familial, from public to personal. When I approach a house, I want to respect and to follow this order so that the house goes beyond shelter to become a reflection of the life cycle. Over time, I have become aware of the deeper and more far-reaching connections within domestic spaces of one kind or another. I strive for houses that are functional but that also reflect the fundamental order of life. The house itself becomes almost animate, with a life of its own. I keep this in mind so that I can bring out the distinguishing features of a particular house as it embodies its version of this chronology.

LEFT

This happy hue stands at attention amid all the scenery.

ABOVE

Daffodils, ignored by the sheep, enjoyed by the guests— what could be more peaceful and serene than this scene?

Formal, Casual, Private Spaces—Inside there are formal and
informal spaces reflecting the differing aspects of the life cycle.
They divide into the formal group of rooms, the casual group, and
the private group, and this division forms the order and whole of a
house. There are spaces for social life, spaces for casual family life,
and spaces for solitude. The formal spaces are the entertaining
spaces, where you invite people to dinner or family lunch or the
club meeting. These are the gathering places in the house, for ease
of bringing people together to eat and talk and socialize. There
are the private spaces for family, the breakfast room or the family
room next to the kitchen. There are spaces that provide solitude,
the library or sitting room or study. And there are personal spaces
to shelter your private self and identity. These divisions
create differing atmospheres, which you can underline
and embody in the choices of configuration of space,
furniture, wall materials, decorative elements, and art.
Will it be wood paneling, paint, or wallpaper? These
design choices create the varied environments and
moods of the formal, casual, and private spaces.

All the rooms fit into the scheme of formal and
casual and private, for sleeping, sitting, eating, or
reading. I like to think of houses as full wardrobes, with
rooms as separate outfits. You can integrate all the parts
of your personality and life into the whole of the house;
it can reflect your sense of humor and creativity, along
with your need to relax alone with a cup of coffee. All
of these spaces and elements become the work of art
that is your dwelling space, reflecting the way you
choose to live. I strive to combine them into a harmony
that encompasses life as a whole—communal moments,
social ones, let-your-hair-down family times, and solitary
downtime. We need all these things from our houses.
Our lives are full, and our houses reflect that variety
and richness.

Hierarchies—I like to underline the hierarchies that are part of this chronology and order by emphasizing certain rooms or features in a house. For example, the front door–back door relationship is a natural hierarchy: the front entrance for guests and social life, the back door for family and house business.

The primacy of the living room is common to all houses. The living room comes first when you are renovating or decorating a house—it's at the top of the hierarchy. It is everyone's choice to do before the other rooms, the place where you put your first and best foot forward. The living room is the public face of the house, our presentable image, even our party or interview look. It's what visitors see when they enter and where you want to impress them most. You probably want to pull out all your stops here—choose the most elegant, opulent fabric for the sofa, find a spectacular Tibetan rug, buy that antique console table you had your eye on.

When I approach the living room, first I give a nod to the architecture. If it needs improvement, I determine if it is feasible and recommend whatever is practical and possible. It is important to ascertain whether an architectural alteration can be achieved structurally. We have to consider how the rooms will connect with each other, the sources of light, and what colors you plan for this room. Are they your favorite colors? Are they the colors of the flowers that come up every year outside the window? Are you picking a neutral palette because there's a collection of art or objects that relates to the color of the room? This is the order: first architecture, then color, and finally windows.

The windows are your strongest point in the room, drawing other elements together the way iron filaments gravitate naturally around a magnet. There are generally two to four windows in any room. Perhaps you also have a fireplace that centers the room, forming a core around which you can orient other features. It can hold things in place, things that would float if the fireplace

An embracing alcove in warm beige and brown tones, from wood furniture to draperies and vases, is a perfect fit to accommodate afternoon tea overlooking the garden, and to draw the room and the landscape together.

LEFT
A formal knot garden easily seen from the living room was designed by the owner.

ABOVE
Art, nature, and artifice blend as this embedded bronze decoration punctuates a wall of rough stones.

PAGE 20, CLOCKWISE FROM TOP LEFT
Greenhouses and a cutting garden outfit the main house on this property. A formal boxwood walkway is part of the exterior aesthetic. The humble traditional Irish cottage, cottage garden, and stone wall create a charming contrast when juxtaposed with the stately main house. The unusual shape of the gate set between the well-tended kitchen and cutting gardens near the house forms an artistic dividing border. It separates and unites these related but distinct indoor and outdoor spaces.

PAGE 21
Exotic palms and a stately chestnut tree share a bike path in a variegated outdoor environment.

were not there, and it gives the right gravity to the room so it doesn't feel scattered or, alternatively, weighed down. I might also hang a chandelier as a prominent eye-catcher, as the jewel in the crown of the room. You can create a vista to another room or an entrance on either side of the fireplace to place the room in the context of the house. Then the house hangs together and is not just a charm bracelet with disparate links. In the living room, I make sure there is something that will lead people to adjacent areas to try out a different space or sink into a different atmosphere, so that the rooms work together and connect. In this way, visitors don't feel stuck in a cubbyhole with no exit.

Balance—Balance is as important as movement in a house. Some of the key elements in the living room can be part of an underlying balance, so that the decor submits to something other than whimsy or practicality. With this perspective in mind, the sofa is not just a place to sit or a pretty piece you found in the store window. It becomes part of an overarching scheme of things that preserves order and balance and has a center and periphery. A pair of bookcases can work miracles of symmetry in a living room, simultaneously framing a fireplace or doorway and adding warmth to the backdrop of painted walls. The living room is the one place that needs more symmetry than others.

I can sense the dynamic of a house as soon as I walk in, and when an element doesn't fit, it feels like an intruder. Your choices of fabric, paint, and furniture work together to produce balance and avoid discord. You don't want your house to be too busy for calm and comfort, which can happen if the colors clash or pile up so you don't know where to focus your attention. You wouldn't put Chinese red upholstery near another equally bright fabric. It's also important to balance variations in tactile sensations and surfaces. I have developed a sensitivity to the tactile aspects of life, which informs my design. If you have a smooth fabric, put something shiny or nubbly against it to animate the surface motion and to balance textures.

ABOVE
Printed linen draperies at the bay window frame the outdoors.

OPPOSITE
The interior view of a rich green library. The wall is accented by multicolored upholstery and an antique carpet.

GEOGRAPHY

The concept of balance is related to the geography of a house.
My favorite house plans for the interior include a center hall that
divides the dining room on one side and the living room on the
other. This plan follows an obvious natural order, and it lends itself
to the simple beauty that resides in the right arrangement and
proportion of things. This is how houses should be. If the dining
room is in the front of the house, the kitchen should be attached
on one side, and if the living room is at the opposite end of the
dining room, the library should be attached on the other side, and
that should make up the first floor—entrance, dining, kitchen,
living, library. All the bedrooms go above. That's the perfect house
and this is a classic plan. This is not an uncommon floor plan in
America—most of my houses have this plan. The house can be
organized from side to side or front to back—both arrangements
are inviting. A house has to have an organization, and this one just
feels right, as if it spontaneously sprang into being to embody the
notion of "house," preordained, from a template of an ideal house.
If a house has this order and geography, you can proceed easily
to choose the furniture and lighting and colors and fabrics to
complement this classic arrangement.

Houses also have geometry. What makes you choose a
circular space for a window looking out on the water? Which
direction does the house face, and how can you make the most
of the views of sunrise or sunset when you configure the rooms
and arrange the furniture? Are you more comfortable with right
angles or with circles? Does this angularity provide a smooth flow,
or is it more staccato than you want it to be?

*Deft handling of scale is obvious in this
generous space, where a Waterford Crystal
chandelier shares quarters with the breakfast
alcove and dining table. The variations of
red in draperies, carpets, and walls unify the
room, emphasizing its scale.*

In the Beginning   25

The classic four-poster beds in this Irish house exaggerate the ceiling height and creates a strong, luxurious architectural statement.

Scale and Space
Inside and Out

When I enter a house, I see the big things first—the overall picture, the ideas, the full-scale map. I see scale and volume, the face of the building, the structure of rooms and ceilings. I look at whether they complement each other. I think about structure, and I think chronologically. What strikes you first as you enter a house?

The medium-size house is the ultimate size because it embraces you. The rooms are not overscaled, so they give you the comfort level of a home. If I am in rooms that are too large, too brightly colored, or too sparsely furnished, I don't get that warm sense of comfort that should envelop me when I open the door. The medium-size house can adjust to your specifications, and you can give it your own twist.

If a house is large, my preference would be to dissect it into smaller spaces so that you get human dimensions. Often the very large mansions that are put up by builders lack detail or are not planned properly, so the scale is disproportionate. If you like a large house because of the location or exterior, you have to be careful to fix the interior scale before you move in, so that when you walk through the front door you are not overwhelmed by exaggerated space. You want your house to enfold the people in it.

You want to walk into a space that feels as if it has the perfect proportion and is not painted a strong color that would be uninviting or forbidding. I don't want to be in garish rooms that feel like a funhouse, or in gaping, cavernous ones, either.

ABOVE
In an example of pairing indoor and outdoor spaces, this glass sunroom connects with nature. Works of art underline this pairing and allow for continuity with the landscape.

RIGHT
A recently added exterior area for dining al fresco overlooking the bay makes the most of the stunning natural setting.

LEFT

Subtle features in a pale cream living room enhance the space. An oversize mirror enlarges the room, and the window seat maximizes family comfort. The room has extended lawn views for connection with the outside. Bookcases flanking the fireplace can accommodate new additions.

OVERLEAF

A long view of the guest house at water's edge.

LEFT
The house interior with a rough-textured overscaled fireplace.

TOP
This lattice overhang provides filtered shade for the brick patio and interior of the house.

ABOVE
A partially enclosed reading deck includes a hot tub (not seen) for an active family.

OVERLEAF
A Long Island house of pale yellow with gray-green shutters.

Variables in architectural scale can change the look of a room
and a house. There is a moment in the architectural design of
houses that allows the architect to do something unexpected—
introduce an overscaled window, like an artist's window, or raise
doors above standard height, or create a view from an upstairs
bedroom into a downstairs hall. The effects of scale work to
alter perspectives and directional lines by shaping space and its
definitions so that your eye sees these variations, although your
brain may not register them explicitly. Your attention is drawn
to linger on a corner or detail, or on a component of the room
that seems compelling, although you don't quite know why.

Novel, interesting spaces arise from geometries and axes
that vary the basics to become newly minted configurations of
architectural fundamentals—that larger window or doorway,
an unexpected view, or a grandly scaled hearth.
Fireplaces are one example of interior elements
that vary in scale and design. Traditional fireplaces
are of traditional height, but there are overscaled
fireplaces in some houses, and in one case the wall
becomes the fireplace. These larger dimensions

TOP RIGHT
*The interior courtyard has entry to the living
room via French doors.*

RIGHT
*On this balcony overlooking the living room,
the cast-iron balustrade matches the lantern
and sconces. The master bedroom opens to
the lower level.*

OPPOSITE
*The fireplace (not seen) centers the furniture
grouping here. The large artist window, an
unexpected element, enlarges the living room
and links it to the outdoors, creating a
variation on architectural basics.*

give pride of place to the fireplace, drawing your eye to it magnetically, allowing it to dominate the room. Scale variations like these can create shifts in temperament, so that drama prevails in one place, a mellow mood in another. They can lend a note of originality to areas of the house that would otherwise have a more conventional look. Things suddenly seem fresh and different. Subliminal details give a house its particularity, its own logic, lifting it from the ordinary.

Plan what is being placed on the walls in terms of scale. Scale can become a problem in interiors—where do you put bigger or smaller pictures, where do you put mirrors, where do you put pairs of mirrors to capture the other room so you see two rooms at once?

I've found you can almost create a formula for placement of mirrors and pictures just by looking at the plan. For example, if there is a fireplace, you have an instant center for a room. It's always nice to flank the fireplace with elements that have visual appeal. You can put mirrors on each side to capture the view of the room behind you or in front of you, or you can place the mirror over the fireplace and put paintings on either side. Mirrors extend and deepen the rooms with their leap into other spaces, and they give a different dimension to the wall, extending its surface into a space that is not visible head-on, the space reflected in them, adding flux between two dimensions and the reflected third one.

If you have a long wall, you want to make sure that it's not going to be bare and boring. Perhaps you want to place a large, epic-proportioned artwork there. Or perhaps a dozen prints of tulips. A collection of small paintings or photographs can offset a larger piece, so that you notice each element and really look, instead of letting your eye glide past. That's when the art

A copper corner fireplace adds charm and eye-catching vigor to this bedroom.

on the walls goes beyond decoration and announces that it deserves attention on its own and isn't just there to fill in a space. A dozen tulips here and a large object there express the dynamic contrast between small and large.

This is the way I give the house a rhythm. Rhythm and balance are important, not just in one room, but throughout the house.

LEFT
Rough-hewn wood walls and a fireplace of randomly set fieldstone feel friendly and comfortable. The fireplace focuses the room visually and wraps it in a cozy atmosphere.

ABOVE
An outdoor fireplace of Connecticut stone is an inspiration, making for an original, dramatic space and giving added character to this unusual columned porch linking landscape with living space.

Respect for Givens

When I approach a house, whether it is newly built, renovated, or needs only a bit of cosmetic surgery, I look at the givens, even if it's a virgin tract of land that hasn't been built on yet. This might entail a gorgeous swath of green, a stand of majestic fir trees, a pond or a brook, or an open expanse of meadows.

If the house is already built and designed, it will exhibit the signature of the architect, which is distinct from that of the interiors. People pick an architect according to their preferences, and this choice reflects the owners in the same way that their designer does. The building may vary according to location, style, and date of original construction. Shingle-style, stucco-inspired Italian villa, rustic retreat, neoclassical, Georgian, and Federal are some style possibilities. I feel that respect for the architecture is

LEFT
Fields on the property become a sculpture garden.

RIGHT
A Donald Kaufman custom color marries this Connecticut house exterior to nature.

PAGE 46
An artist uses local elements lifted from the land and made into art to enhance and decorate the landscape of the property.

PAGE 47
A bold stroke of invention shaped the foundation of an old structure on this property to fashion a swimming pool.

OPPOSITE
Built originally as a great room in the 1930s, this one was refurbished to accommodate large dinner parties and entertaining.

ABOVE
Pine paneling, doors, and railings are part of the architectural grammar that lends this house its particular look.

RIGHT
A bird's-eye view of the master bedroom. There is nothing like a freshly made bed.

of critical importance. Sometimes I'll find that earlier designers didn't have that respect, and they placed screens against walls or covered fireplaces.

The elements I begin with are crucial to the outcome. This is the stage set. The history and evolution of the house influence the design at the outset—it is not just a matter of what you can do with the interiors. The mix of elements—the architecture, the lives of the clients, the landscape, and particular features like that natural wonder of mature trees—forms the integrity not only of the setting but also of the design and of the concept of the whole.

The key word is respect. *I respect the natural environment, I respect the lives of the clients and their choice of architects, I respect the genius and skill of those architects. The choices I make reflect this mix. As with any project that is an act of creation, these are the raw materials, the canvas and palette, without which the project would not exist.*

As a designer I am not interested in calling attention to myself—I feel grateful for the materials that present themselves to me and for the opportunity to work with them. It may seem like a paradox, but working within parameters gives me a feeling of freedom to create, to let my mind and instincts grapple with the challenge of playing with what is there, without working against it. The givens are absolutes within which to create, and they are the riches I feel privileged to inherit when I start a project.

ABOVE
The combination of the Prussian blue color used on the exterior of this studio house and the lead-coated copper roof make a bold statement appropriate to its artistic purpose. A stone sculpture and a metal sculpture by the owner complement the house.

OPPOSITE
The artist's window looking into the woods is an example of the unusual effect of scale an architect can create.

The interior of an owner's studio, with mid-century modern sofa and chairs. Architecture serves art—a stone fireplace and wainscoting display prints and model studies.

RIGHT
Pine kitchen cabinets, chairs, and tables outfit this country kitchen. The beamed ceiling, stove, stone floors, and display shelves of china add pattern and color.

In every house, I take the basket of givens and use its contents as building blocks for the whole. I love the adventure and challenge of getting the blend of architecture, nature, and lifestyle choices right, so that the clients are happy in the house and it reflects them. The design is influenced by the requirements and the vision and the expectation of the client. In designing these houses, my mission is to respect a particular house in a specific location by a particular architect in a given time for a specific family. It's a communal undertaking. From that blend, a natural harmony arises.

It's like a recipe: you take a bit of respect, you freshen things up and make them a bit more compatible with the client or the location or the year in which we are living, and you end up with the particularity that makes each individual house its own.

MORE THAN
THE SUM OF ROOMS

A House Is a Whole and a Home

A house is a symphony, not a chamber piece. As designer, I am sometimes the composer and sometimes the conductor of the symphony. I try to bring the parts together, going beyond the physical house to make it a home.

There is an element of planning with a house that doesn't happen with a room. The scale is larger, and it's a bigger endeavor to organize a house so that it flows properly. Every house has its own continuity and consistency, even when the elements are eclectic, its own version of miscellany cohering into order. The rooms are not just jumbles of furniture and shapes and colors. They come together not only to express an aesthetic, but also to create a mood.

*Handsome Chinese tables and vases anchor this space,
which is a passage to an appealing wood-paneled library.*

My living room might contain luxurious things, but it feels warm and comforting.

What makes a house more than the sum of its rooms? A room is a unit of space and shelter, and it is a basic necessity, a fact of life. Rooms are like simple utensils or measurements, a spoon or a yardstick. We think in these units, and we need them for the task at hand—living. Houses are all-encompassing, full expressions of their inhabitants, coats of many colors. They go beyond necessity to choice and elaboration. I enjoy giving play to the various aspects of houses, past and present, part and whole, necessity and invention.

Repetition and the Relation of the Rooms to the House—
When I think about the relation of the rooms to the house, I know that the rooms have to be respectful of and complementary to each other. The rooms are not separate from each other. Each room has to relate to the house and to the other rooms. You are not jumping from one aesthetic to another—there's a flow to the design as well as to the physical pattern of movement from room to room. You want to create not only an aesthetic but an invitation, to maximize the enjoyment of all the rooms. Houses have to be as integrated as a single room. The parts have to equal the sum of the house, just as the parts of a room have to equal the sum of its space. A house requires a wide-angle lens.

What makes for continuity? To pull the house together, I repeat motifs. In the living room, I draw you to the next room and through the house in slow motion, linking the family of rooms. Wooden chairs in the living room and wood in the library pick up the thread leading you from one room to the next. You should not need a legend to go from room to room.

RIGHT
The grand proportions of this room showcase an art collection and various amply sized furniture groupings. The French doors leading to a beautiful terrace open the boundaries of the space to the outside.

OVERLEAF
A single, well-placed painting picks up the color of the coffee tables to bring focus to the main seating.

There's always a reason to reference one aspect of the house to another. It's not only a memory point, it actually takes you from one space to another without a confusing journey. A blue rug goes to the blue in a painting. You might not realize it, but you are subconsciously affected by the repetitions and reminders, which make for easy transitions from room to room and create a harmony that affects your response to the surroundings.

Balance resides in the repetitions, too. As you go from one room to another, if you do not repeat the color on the walls, the color you choose, contrasting or neutral, can provide balance. One choice I make to preserve balance is to bring the color of the walls into an accessory in another room. Or if two rooms are very close in character, sometimes I like to make the draperies from the same fabric. A brilliant primary color might draw you away from the room in a distracting way, creating imbalance. If rooms are horizontally connected, and there is an open view from living room on one end to dining room on the other, the choice of color and materials can anchor this balance. I might keep the curtains the same and change the color of the upholstery. This will emphasize the directional lines and add gravity to spatial shifts. Balance equals continuity.

Flow and Movement—In a house, I want to facilitate movement. The house flows from living room to dining room. When visitors arrive at the house, cocktails in the living room are followed by dinner. If I have a terra-cotta color for the pillows on the sofa in the living room, then I might use it on the dining room walls.

An accent in one room becomes a major element in another, and the place springs to life in a sprightly way. The color of the carpet at the entrance is replayed in a painting, and honey-colored furniture goes from one place to the other. That room you can see from the living room, whether it is a study or

library or sitting room or porch, can beckon with echoes to entice you from one space to another, to encourage you to try it out here and there, for variety. These echoes make for a soothing, continuous movement from room to room, shifting motifs but nothing abrupt, no shocks in temperament or sensibility. You don't want discordant jolts from rooms that don't belong together under one roof and violate the essence of the house. The repetitions are subtle transitions that eliminate choppiness. The motion from room to room should feel natural, but with a hint of novelty, like a new outfit that gives you a lift.

The furniture should underline the divisions of space and its flow. When you look into another room, you want to see furniture that calls out to you to experience that room. Why don't I take my coffee to that window in the morning and sit by that desk in that alcove in that cozy chair? A mix of sofa and chairs feels inviting. The chairs have to be comfortable. To be interesting, the furniture and upholstery in the formal rooms must cause your guests to know that they are in your house and that this is your personal style. The furniture contributes to the creation of atmosphere in the rooms and to the overall dynamic and movement in the house.

LEFT
The dining porch features a fireplace, beautiful light, and vistas.

RIGHT
Shading the sitting area adjacent to the pool, this striking pergola adds its own artistry to the exterior space of this house.

You want to create vistas that encourage you to be in all the rooms of the house, whether for entertaining or for personal purposes. The alcove by the desk in the library is a more casual family space, perhaps for that cup of coffee. It is not about entertaining, but a visitor might be led there irresistibly from the living room by a view of marvelous old volumes with the weathered richness of antiquity, with a whiff of history and quiet contemplation. You do want people to be curious enough to venture toward that lovely room where they can retreat with a book, for a new experience that is part of the casual life of the house but that is not off-limits from the more formal areas. The library might also come in handy as a specialty area for conversation and dessert. Spaces in houses are not for limited access, and you don't want your spaces to have a no-visitors feeling. When the space is right, it invites exploration.

For practicality, furniture needs to be kept out of the traffic patterns in your home. Properly placed furniture leads you through the house and creates a sense of movement. The size of the rugs has to follow the path from one room to the other. You don't want to trip on the corner of a rug every time you go from room to room,

so the scale of the carpet or area rug is a factor to be measured and planned carefully.

Stairways underline flow and movement, and they give physical form to the geographic relationship of formal and private spaces. Stairways are part of the natural order in houses. They sweep your eye upward to the private areas from the formal parts of the house that are for visitors, reminding us that this is, after all, not a public space but a private house, where living happens on multiple levels, literally and metaphorically. Stairways punctuate the house, separating its levels and also bringing them together, dividing upstairs and downstairs and linking them. A rectangular staircase feels orderly and neat, and a circular one can lend excitement and vibrancy to the exchange of upstairs and down. Beautiful staircases captivate the eye.

Flow and movement make the house come alive. When I walk into a house that doesn't have this dynamic, it feels static and heavy—it stands still. I need to feel that the house has life in it and is not frozen in time or space.

TOP

A rectangular staircase has its own measured geometry and tempo. This one benefits from lines emphasizing angles as well as the softer curves of the banister as it rounds at the bottom. The vertical stripes in the rag carpet create a visual path. The bronze frog contemplating an artwork by Robert Mangold adds a whimsical note.

RIGHT AND OPPOSITE

This beautiful organic staircase showcases a client's carved bald eagle and metal Indian sculpture.

CHARACTER OF ROOMS
AND THEIR PLACE IN THE HOUSE

DINING ROOM

The dining room is for entertaining—part of the formal space. Social life has shifted somewhat, from the days when the dining room was used for family, to its role as a room for gatherings. It is a night room, partly because of the role of the breakfast room, which was created in this country and now exists in Europe, too. With the increasing use of breakfast rooms, the dining room is for Sunday lunch or brunch and dinner. It is often enclosed, and on the dark side of the house. The most important decision is to bring color in to animate what could be a dark space, whether it is on the walls or upholstery or table and chairs. I have fun by exaggerating the color, using a color from another area and putting it on the walls. I always choose proper lighting that will create a feeling of ease and elegance. I am also careful in my choice of dining-table surfaces, draperies, rugs, and chair fabrics, which should be aesthetically appealing as well as practical, allowing for inevitable spills.

I like to put amusing things on the dining room walls that guests can spy from other rooms. I am always conscious of the perimeter of the dining room and how it interacts with the rest of the interior and exterior. When you are sitting at the dining table, don't you want to see something lovely?

Mirrors activate walls and rooms by collecting and reflecting light, which is important in enlivening the dining room at night.

I always try to play with mirrors in a dining room—and art. If you place a mirror opposite the window, you will capture the outside view in the daytime. You can juxtapose mirrors with art, so that when you walk inside you see a painting on the opposite wall reflected in the mirror. This creates an energetic play of real and reflected, palpable and illusory. It's a flight of fancy!

The warmth of red bathes this dining alcove, drawing together the chairs, lamps, table linens, furniture appointments, and the pièce de résistance, a painting purchased in France.

Kitchen—I have always thought of the kitchen, which is part of the casual family area, as the heart of the home, starting from my childhood sense that it was full of family life. I want to be sure it works for family interaction, even though I organize it primarily as a workable space for cooking. Barstools are essential as casual perches for an impromptu chat. I also like to add some beautiful things to look at, so that the kitchen has an inviting aesthetic. One of the kitchens I designed has shelves of hotel silver, and copper fixtures over the island. The silver and copper, along with the porcelain-topped table, are all distinctive finishes that make the surfaces dance.

You will have kitchen design choices that range from conventional to modern. They require more than good proportions and natural light. Whether you are building or renovating your kitchen, choosing color, style, and appliances can be overwhelming. Kitchen consultants, architects, and designers are useful, with their greater experience, but be ever aware of your own expectations and avoid following whatever fashion is trendy. Classic style has a longer life, and simple design can be adjusted without a major renovation.

HERE ARE SOME GUIDELINES

■ Choose a suitable layout. How will it work best for your food preparation needs?

■ Visit appliance showrooms and cabinet shops to get an idea of the range and variety of choices.

■ Investigate stone and other materials for counters and floors.

■ Be aware of light sources and opportunities for outside views.

OPPOSITE TOP
Modern materials, stainless steel, and a glass tile backsplash enhance this working kitchen. The hanging lights are by Philippe Stark.

OPPOSITE BOTTOM
The placement of this boathouse kitchen takes advantage of its location near the water's edge. With its breakfast table and country French chairs, it is perfect for a family gathering.

ABOVE
Chatting and fixing food coexist nicely in this crisp white eat-in kitchen, with its refreshing country feel.

The master four-poster bed is reflected in the overscaled mirror next to the window to the outside, so that your gaze fluctuates between landscape and room.

Softly draped vanilla silk adds scale to the master bedroom, with its view of an interesting tree from an inviting bed. I favor white sheets and shams for a clean, comfortable look.

The Private Rooms—Master bedrooms are about the comfort of the bed and its relationship to the outdoors. I like to position the bed so that you can see something you love from it, or something beautiful, not just the utilitarian area of the bathroom. Maybe the bed will face the ocean or a favorite tree that flowers every year. If your bed must face a bathroom and dressing room, you want to have a view that is appealing to the eye. You want to see the attractive sides of the dressing room, closets, and bathroom.

Bathrooms—You should not pick loud colors or complicated tile patterns—they can get tiresome. Choose colors you can live with, and pick your finishes wisely. Make sure your bathroom has good tile or marble, well-made cabinetwork, and quality fixtures and fittings. Although the bathroom needs to be serviceable, it should be attractive.

ABOVE
Textural and visual delights combine in faux bamboo ceramic tile, teak cabinetry, and marble countertops in this bathroom.

RIGHT
Why not put a fantastic limestone fireplace in the master bathroom so you can enjoy it from the soaking tub?

Children's Rooms—Children's rooms require their own mind-set. In designing them, I look in my bag of tricks for solutions that go with the territory. I adjust my expectations toward the controlled chaos end of the spectrum, and I try to have realistic goals. Children's rooms have their own special-interest design choices. Your preferences can prevail up to a point, but all of us with children know that there are limits on governing the ways and the look of our descendants. In the lives of children, unruly nature does not always submit to decor. Still, with children's rooms I strive for a measure of visual pleasure tempered by the freedom we have an obligation to give to our children, and of order tempered by the certainty that things will not be in order all the time.

I might choose a storage area for toys and clothes that is both practical and attractive—boxes or drawers or handsome shelves or cabinets—in your child's favorite color or with an original design fillip. The shelves can be organized in a grid of cubbies that will submit a messy tumble to a pleasing look. This gives interest to functional furnishings that are necessary equipment. I keep in mind that lessons in keeping order can be learned when the child is given responsibility for his or her own space. Since children's clothing stacks more than hangs, the shelves serve a double purpose. When a young child puts his or her animals on shelves haphazardly, that grid of shelves or receptacles can turn the carnival into an attractive visual ground. Later, playthings can make way for books and other objects for the maturing child.

I am mindful that children's rooms are about the child, but not in an intrusive way vis-à-vis the house. At issue are the location of the rooms and the view they present to grown-ups. I like to make sure that the children's rooms are part of the movement and flow of the rest of the house and not a separate offshore island. If we put a blue print on the bedspread in your child's room, let's echo it by hanging a picture with blue in it in the hallway outside the room.

BELOW
Matching spool beds, quilts in primary colors, and a background of sprightly patterned striped and flowered wallpaper provide lively notes for a young lady's room.

OPPOSITE
This French bed deserves center stage in a lovely bedroom.

SOME USEFUL KEYS TO A SUCCESSFUL CHILD'S ROOM ARE THE FOLLOWING:

■ You will have to adjust the bed size, from a single child's bed for a youngster up to the age of ten or twelve, to a full or queen size thereafter. One important factor for our social children: for sleepover provision, two twins might work, or you may prefer a pullout bed. And there are always sleeping bags.

■ An attractive desk or work surface, with computer access, is necessary in our high-tech, wired world, the world our kids know better than we do.

■ I always emphasize floor space for playing. I choose area carpets for practical reasons. They are easier to replace than wall-to-wall when there is unforeseen damage or when style preferences change as your child grows. I like paint better than wallpaper, also for reasons of expediency. Paint is easier to update than wallpaper. If you do insist on wallpaper, be sure to choose a design that will endure through age changes. For these areas, I also recommend poster art that can be framed to preserve the longevity of the walls.

Wallpaper adds texture, and the American four-poster bed feels solid in a child's room. Blue textiles on the bed and chair are echoed in the blue of a painting outside, linking the room with the rest of the house.

4

PAST AND PRESENT

Stories

You may not have given much thought to the house beyond its existence as a physical object. But every house has stories, of its character and of its creation and of its history. If you become aware of the house as concept and as story, this can add to its richness as you outfit it with features that express the varied lives within. Then, when you walk into it with your arms full of groceries and you get a wonderful feeling of home, the house is speaking to you with its own voice, the voice that echoes with stories and life, past and present. Think of the house in *To the Lighthouse,* a house that Virginia Woolf describes in human terms, as if it were a person who has seen life and has experienced

The front entrance showcases some fundamentals of the house:
original wide-plank pine floors and the plain beauty of the stair and its railing.

The tidy stone walkway is bordered with a boxwood hedge. A stone dog with a quizzical expression guards the porch.

Floor-length windows flank the chimney in the library addition.

Crisp white painted shingles with almost black shutters and cedar roof make this house proud.

the pains and pleasures of a sentient being. Houses live and breathe with the lives within. They are animated with their stories. The flip side of plans and design choices is this intangible side. It is the underpinning of what you apprehend with your senses.

Treasures and Memorabilia—I often use memorabilia as an enriching domestic feature. Each object tells its story in a particular form and shape and color, and you can feel memories and meaning drifting up from these talismans from the past. Anything you love, that old column from the flea market, or a firehouse-red photo of tulips against a starry sky, can be part of the blend. You can put things together judiciously so that they fit. I love it when I walk into a house and feel that the past is present and palpable. My Remsenburg house is mature now, and you can see my treasures in it, some old faces, old friends, reused. That's a good thing when it comes to a house—it means that you are able to bring some of yourself to the new circumstances. Even in a house that is new for a family, that rocking horse near the fireplace has a story I want to hear. These voices and whispers from the past bring dimensions beyond the material and physical and tactile surfaces, and beyond design elements like color and texture. Our houses are all treasure chests. Your objects—that painted iron firewood bin from your childhood home, a porcelain cake plate—are not just tangible artifacts or aesthetic pieces with sensuous surfaces. Lives are held in them. Beauty and meaning fuse, lifting your house from the ordinary toward something more lasting.

BELOW
The sparsely furnished front hall is home to a few cherished possessions, longtime members of the family: the chairs, table, lantern, and portrait, each with its own story from my heritage.

OPPOSITE
Well-chosen objects create harmony with this painting of a Long Island field.

OVERLEAF
The painting, by Shanaz Said, mimics the tall windows and fills the corner. White walls and upholstery keep the room loose and airy, and a huge bunch of white hydrangeas adds a floral grace note. The saw on the table loses its threat when you see that it displays a gorgeous landscape painting on its blade.

I have a huge collection of cookie jars that I started back in the sixties, twenty or thirty of them. I was intrigued by these old-fashioned ceramics, which were probably for biscuits. Some of them were painted to look like houses, and this refers to the many stories of houses in my life, the houses of my family in our small town and the story of my choosing to design houses. I love to cook and bake, as all the women I grew up with did. They all made hors d'oeuvres and cookies and cakes that people would buy for parties. Although they weren't allowed to have a profession or job, most of the women were industrious. They were skilled seamstresses, and they knitted and crocheted. They were the children of late Victorians, the women Washington Irving described as having "scissors and pincushions" in their pockets. The cookie jars are emblematic of that era and of the women under whose aprons I grew up and learned to provision and embellish a house and a life. These folksy crockery houses are part of the memory bank of my childhood in the American Midwest. It is from there that my cozy, livable design approach emerges.

I have antique bed linens and quilts—they are American quilts, grandmother's attic ephemera. I have one called a Plain Quilt—it's blue and white and it's on my bed. I have never reupholstered many of the things I've bought over the years. I fall in love with the fabric, and I don't change that fabric. I use the things that I love. I don't regard them as show objects, for display as if in a museum. They are the appointments of my home, and they have my affection and my everyday fidelity. They surround the small necessities and routines of domestic life with beauty and with historic resonance. In my house they are put to use as paraphernalia, at once serviceable, endearing, pleasing to the eye, and replete with our collective American memory. They are homespun finds from our national past, and they are also tagged with my origins. These things form my private arsenal, for use and for the pleasure of finding beauty in the practical, the everyday.

OPPOSITE
This corner was an opportunity for a black-and-white moment showcasing a collection of white stoneware and an unmatched set of French chairs.

OVERLEAF
The subtle use of color values visually connects the library, dining hall, and living room. All spaces are regularly used by my family and friends.

BELOW

The "Pink" cottage.

OPPOSITE

Striped wallpaper on the ceiling tents this sunroom, adding character to a tiny space and opening it out. The use of pink gives it personality.

PAGE 98

The consistency of color scheme in matching fabric and wallpaper is a space extender here, too.

PAGE 99

The juxtaposition of window and mirror enlivens this room by adding unseen views, enlarging the space. The continuity of the pink palette expands the cottage.

Inner Life and Spirit—Inanimate objects, chairs and fixtures, art, and accessories can impart animation and amusement to your house, adding to the spirit within.

I hang mobiles in my houses in unexpected places—over the dining table or staircase, for example—for a diverting, playful note. Your eye is drawn upward over the elegant dining table, and what do you see? Ah, a mobile. It winks at you, and you smile back. Mobiles are a touch of fantasy. Upholstery trimmings can be part of the romp—I have put fanciful tassels on the arms of white armchairs, which otherwise might retreat into a benign, neutral background. Your eye fixes on these dangling tassels, a jaunty dollop of joy on a chair. The furniture isn't so serious, after all.

In my house, I have fifty-five chairs, and that in itself is a story. One of my friends asked if I knew how many chairs I own and started counting. I have chairs everywhere, sets of chairs, pairs of chairs, single chairs, chairs on the landing, chairs in the rooms, chairs everywhere. They are like people. They are my friends. I love them. This is the invisible life of the chairs. If you look in a room, you'll see—there's a pair, there's a pair, there's a pair. There are French ones that I had reupholstered, and they are not in the right

fabric. The color is off, but they are what they are. That's one peculiar chair tale. Each chair is its own character in a chair world.

Unusual trimmings or art that is bold add to this spirit of fun and liveliness. One wall has a painting that is a silvery circle drawn in irregular concentric swirls, like a doodle or a loosely wound skein of yarn. This is not laugh-out-loud humor—it's more of a chuckle. There may be a corner of a bookcase dedicated to things you found on your nature walk, or a wall of children's drawings, artfully framed and arranged so that you have to look again, examining them at close range to see what they really are. We are all familiar with these wonderful duplicities on our walls or coffee table, and they may even fool and delight some self-proclaimed sophisticates.

For a long time I have collected art without rhyme or reason, according to whim. Some of it is modern, some less so, and I care about it all. An artwork I love is by John Okulick. It is on the table next to a window in the country. It represents the bird I love to look at. From the sunroom in Remsenburg I've been watching the extraordinary variety of birds on Long Island, and in my library I have books on birds. The Okulick is a sculpture of a bird looking at a drawing of twigs on a tree as if the bird were a spectator, tree-watching the way people bird-watch. It's a gentle joke, a rejoinder to our nature-loving, as if the bird says, Okay, I can look, too. I love it that it is a botanical that isn't quite—it's a riff on a botanical. It is as if I gave the artist my favorite from a conventional series of birds and foliage and ferns and said, Do something with this. That's the story this work tells.

The things in our houses spin our yarns. The cookie jars that are part and parcel of the look of my present house prove how much the past of houses lives in their present, no matter how sophisticated and up-to-date the house might be. These things tell of the merging of then and now. I like to blend the coziness of grassroots artifacts with the sophistication and elegance of what we think of as "art," to assemble contrasting things in a way that works. I have my cookie jars and my library with the books I

BELOW
A country bathroom is more like a room, with the sink in an old French sideboard, drawings, and a favorite upholstered chair and stool.

OPPOSITE
My Okulick bird is fun, an inverted comment on nature-watching—the bird sculpture watches birds. This is twinkle-in-the-eye humor, giving a lift because it surprises. The khaki-and-white color scheme as a modern approach replaces a dark period standard option.

OVERLEAF
In this room the soft white and blue palette provides the perfect balance for the pine floor. A few of my various beloved chairs populate the room.

This house is built on a hill, with terraced steps leading to the front entrance.

The front hall's patterned tile floor, column, and stair window are part of the original architecture.

The book collection in the library tells of the owner's travels and other varied interests. The library furniture expresses refinement, adventure, and historic resonance, a step into a realm of stories from everywhere. An arched window looks to the outside world. This room is an inviting, elegant, and appropriate blend of past and present, near and far.

The overall view of the living room is anchored by a beautiful antique carpet.

The fireplace wall in this living room is open to the library in a user-friendly way, creating a vista that encourages exploration of a different space.

collected for my children, and my fifty-five chairs that are like people, and my sculpture of a bird watching a tree. I need to have my things around me. They speak to me in their own tongues. They become the fabric of my life, as do yours. You put them in the house, and the house becomes a vessel, an anthology of tales.

In my bathroom I have a collection of gold-rimmed cups for bathroom materials, cotton and Q-tips, and so forth. One of the cups is a precious keepsake from childhood, with my mother's name scrolled in gold. When I look at that cup every day, my mother is there with me. She would have been happy that I am using her cup still, and that it holds useful things, everyday things. It speaks from her life and now from mine and combines them, and that makes me feel that the past moves into the present in a good way, in the form of a gold-rimmed cup with its soft note of antiquity, its old-fashioned patina of remembrance.

BELOW

The dressing and bath areas are well organized and outfitted to the owners' needs. They contain treasures, each its own work of art—gold-topped jars, a stunningly framed mirror with unusual geometric border design, and crystal lamps in curved and spiral shapes, with a jewel-like quality. The artistic placement of these objects in this functional space infuses the room with personality.

OPPOSITE

The master bedroom is meant to be a quiet oasis. This is a perfect example, with its sitting room, soft coloring, and exterior vistas.

The colorful past and vital present, the treasures and stories of a house, along with its chronology—its own version of the life cycle, and with the way its geography reflects its inhabitants—these show that houses have inner as well as outer lives, soul and spirit as well as design and construction. There's diversity of style in these houses, but a house isn't itself just because it has a particular style. The inner life of the house gives it its moods and its qualities, its bustle and calm and intimacy. Without this inner life the house would be sterile, cold, a blank space with walls and chairs and tables. The inner life is the uplift, from chairs and walls to a living space that is alive. With it, with the spirit and animation, and with the humor that suffuses its atmosphere through touches of whim and whimsy, each house has a distinct personality and sensibility.

TOP RIGHT
These family room bookcases display wooden stationery boxes and other folk art objects, for a note of historic richness and a feeling of timelessness. Antique pewter tankards in graduated sizes are displayed on the mahogany table.

RIGHT
Light enters this hallway, reflecting off an Early American painted piece and a hoop-back Windsor chair. The American folk past asserts itself in these objects, and the weathered blue paint adds vivaciousness to the room.

OPPOSITE
The hallway serves as a gallery for a painted wooden cabinet with colorful folk motifs and cosmic symbols and for a rocking chair studded with stars and circles, perhaps with magical connotations, perhaps with a connection to the spirit world. These are one-of-a-kind antique American folk art pieces telling tales from our homespun history.

5

CONCEAL AND REVEAL

Houses are both open and shut places. They conceal the life within and they shelter it, and they open their doors to reveal it, to share its spirit with visitors. Doors and windows are the physical punctuation for these two faces of house life, concealing and revealing. They embody those opposing states of being as they perform the actions of opening and closing. Windows look out and reveal, doors are for privacy, to close and open at will. They conceal and reveal the inhabitants of the house, literally, and parallel to that, they conceal and reveal as they allow light to enter, or filter it or shade us from it, or shut it out. Light and dark are the natural phenomena that conceal and reveal. They are critical to the aesthetic and mood of a house. Light rooms, dark rooms, day rooms, night rooms—we need these variations to live out the shifting moments of our lives.

Hallway passages at the front entrance link various rooms,
allowing for roaming and retreat.

Sometimes we want to be flooded with light. At other times, the same people who want to live only in bright places love the dark of night, its mysteries and quiet and enveloping quality, perhaps in a room that wraps itself around you like a quilt. There can be appropriate places in a house for light and dark. Think of the library and the sunroom. Concealing and revealing, opening and closing, and illuminating and darkening pervade what houses are about. I always think in terms of this double nature of houses as I work on them.

Siting—The siting of the house, where it sits on the lot, acreage, or estate, is important as its platform. Siting affects light and views; it determines how you see nature from and around the house, which angles will allow the house to get the most out of its environment. Siting will affect the specifics of the interior, influencing the choice of day and night rooms. I take the site into account in designing interiors and outdoor spaces.

Doors—Doors are major features in the geography of the house, leading from without to within, delineating areas for social and familial life, and separating the public and private spaces by serving as crossing points and barriers. From your house you can walk out through the front door to nature, as you would not be able to do in an apartment. Doors also play a part in the chronology of the house, the various stages of life. We know that young children want their doors open at night for a feeling of security. We have all lived with the perennially closed door of an adolescent, or the noisily exposed room of a music enthusiast, or the use of a door as a statement, slammed or closed gently. Doors can be instruments of expression and communication, metaphors for welcoming or keeping out. As people grow and change, the open or closed door, the firmly closed door, and the door open a crack all reflect something about lives at certain ages and stages.

You want guests to come in through the front door, not via the kitchen or back door, so they get the effect of the natural setting and see the best of the house first. Perhaps you have chosen a glass door leading to glass French doors at the other end, so the view is a clean sweep, with momentum all the way through the house, bestowing transparency and openness like a breeze blowing through the house, with vistas from the front door to the back. But at night, you might not want that front door to be all glass. One solution I recommend is an outside door and an inside door, or the classic architectural solution: a solid door with glass sidelights.

Inside the house, conceal and reveal is played out in passageways as you move into the house and among rooms, with doors marking points along the way, lookout points. There are various arteries, halls for free roaming leading to rooms for retreat, and they are embellished by the doors, which are decorative and design elements as well as functional ones. They close and open for privacy and availability, and they draw the eye with their materials and design and colors. Door choices indoors and out can include glass or a combination of materials, wood or metal. They can be rough-hewn or refined. There are old-world heavy metal doors with locks and studs, wood-paneled doors, and painted farm doors with metal hinges.

THE SCREEN DOOR: Let's not forget the charm of a screen door, the reminiscence of a screen door. The screen door is an American classic, often accompanying the porch as a feature of the American domestic-built environment, a historic folk element and a practical one. It can be overlooked, or at least out of focus. It is found in country houses more than in suburban areas, and it comes in differing styles, historic

BELOW
These country door frames, appealing for their simplicity, are from America's grass-roots idiom.

OPPOSITE
The gate-enclosed porch entrance to a Hampton ocean-side shingle-style house constitutes a singular point of arrival.

and handcrafted, with or without carved inserts. It mediates the move from exterior to interior in its special way, and although it does not confer privacy, it allows for light and openness to the landscape at the same time that it provides a demarcation from it, keeps unwanted wildlife away, and discourages unannounced visitors. To appreciate its subtle place in human interaction, imagine a conversation through a screen door. The quality of the interchange is altered because there is a door in between, a gentle don't-get-too-close gesture, especially if there is a deliberate decision to keep the screen door shut but talk through it. The screen door is an unsung invention with multiple virtues.

Windows—Windows are mediators of light. They manage the flux between the interior and the exterior. Houses come alive because of windows. You should always maximize windows to get the light through, so that they breathe in the light. You don't want to cover them up. When I address the inside of a house, I don't want to negate the outside, I want to accentuate it, embrace it. Large expanses or small amounts of glass, or glazing as it is called in the building industry, permit the natural light to enter and open the interior to nature. The quantity of glass should be in accord with the style of architecture.

PRIVACY AND LIGHT, A DILEMMA: Windows bring the outside in, so that the house is part of it, but the windows come with decisions. If there is a substantial number of windows in the house, how do you get privacy? When what you see is good, that is a desirable solution to the lookout dilemma. An ugly building or an immediate neighbor is not. But there are tricks we use to fool the light and dark problem and resolve the coexistence of privacy and light.

ABOVE
An Alexander Calder sculpture replaces the need for any window treatment.

OPPOSITE
An iron sculpture by the owner of this attractive house harmonizes with the view of the bay overlooking the ocean, adding art to the setting.

PAGE 124
The vaulted high ceiling and clerestory windows maximize light and views. Colors are neutral to accentuate the total atmosphere of this room.

PAGE 125
The all-neutral white palette is always a great backdrop for an art collection.

A European country-style kitchen often mixes paint and wood, evoking comfort along with utility.

WINDOW SHADES, SHUTTERS, AND BLINDS: Shutters were the classic way to have air without direct sun. Victorian houses had shutters that closed. Houses in the South had outside shutters that functioned as architectural elements. Interior shutters exist in brownstones—they have a paneled side that goes into the reveal, so that the panel works with the window jamb and the other wooden details around the window. When you open it, it pushes back into the reveal. Horizontal blinds started in the fifties as wood blinds with tapes, and now they can be thinner, with strings. They can be adjusted to control the light without entirely shutting out the view.

Solar screen shades, shutters, or blinds cut down the light and allow you to see a reduced image of the exterior. Tinted glass, in its many new versions, can admit rays in varying percentages. Glass curtains, sheers, or "nets," as the English call them, are also a graceful glare reducer, to draw at high noon. They are translucent or transparent materials that, when gathered, give you privacy, functioning as curtains. When they are open, they stack on the sides. On the ground level, should you want privacy, use a drapery panel that dresses the window, and then add sheer curtains that close so there is still light coming through. In this way we borrow light without giving up to total glass.

Solar screens are a wonderful replacement for the old-fashioned roller shades or curtains you draw. An image from outside comes through the shade and forms a shadowy painting in the window, a trompe l'oeil effect, but it doesn't block the light. You can purchase these shades with greater or lesser density—even with greater density, you still have light. The scene outside can become part of your environment, whether it is architectural, natural, or agrarian.

RIGHT
At one end of the living room, the entire wall becomes the fireplace. The color of the stone was used for textured upholstery and carpet, uniting the room seamlessly.

OVERLEAF
The master bedroom has direct access to the outdoors with floor-to-ceiling windows and glass doors opening to the outside. The monochromatic color scheme has been chosen to create a restful retreat.

My apartment in New York feels and behaves like a house. From the windows I see a small orange house, a strange apparition in the big city. It forms an image through the shade, along with the decorative redbrick building next to it, and the whole scene framed in the solar shade creates a fairy-tale effect.

Houses on ground level have a circumstantial duality, a double vision, enjoying the exterior and exposing the interior. In winter, when it gets dark at four thirty, windows turn into black spaces, and you may not want to draw curtains and make a wall where there is a window. You might consider exterior lighting. Then the blackness becomes a starry night, with a light-dark tableau animating the outside and the interior: a backdrop with a galaxy of light. I like the excitement of glitter in darkness, the sparkle of light in the night.

Day and night, you do want what you look at outside the window to be beautiful. Houses have land around them so that you do not look directly at other houses. We want access to the blue sky and the light and the sun that make us feel warm and comfortable. If your landscape is attractive, it forms the scenic backdrop for your dwelling, the landscape painting offsetting the domestic miniatures of your interiors.

ARCHITECTURE can also be put to work in controlling the intensity of light. One of the ways to reduce intense light is to have an overhang on the house. It may become a porch or remain a simple overhang, and it typifies exteriors in warmer regions of the globe. It can make the interior a bit darker, but it will be cooler, which is desirable in the tropics. As an architectural element, the area where the roof extends downward can be an aesthetic feature of the exterior of the house, as well as useful for diminishing light and heat.

Windows by day, doors by night! Three arched doorways lead from the garden to an evening dinner.

Artificial Lighting—Light and dark conceal and reveal just as doors do. Natural light is outdoorsy and outgoing, lamps are cozy and intimate, and chandeliers are partygoers. Some people prefer the frankness of spotlights or bright lights, others like a lamplight glow, and still others a more monastic or romantic twilight dimness, but not gloom. Lamps shed light at human height, wrapping people in a domestic embrace. Overhead lights can spread brightness around, encouraging social interchange and goodwill. With dimmers, they can adjust to the amount of light you want. I like to vary the lighting to delineate spaces, to set off the social and familial spaces from the quiet corners. I can create a mood just by choosing the hue of a lampshade to vary the tint of

LEFT

The focus of this crisp white dining room is its overscale refectory table surrounded by comfortable chairs designed especially for it. The delicacy of the iron chandelier lightens the room.

OPPOSITE

The antique table was purchased by the owners on holiday in Bali. The chairs are from the Mariette Himes Gomez Private Label Collection. The leather screen is a decorative nod to the West.

PAGE 136

In the hall looking toward the master bedroom, the cool feeling of a white color scheme works well for the location at the beach.

PAGE 137

White bed covers always look clean and fresh. Even better is an all-white bed.

the light, or by the placement of ceiling lights to illuminate one place or another for sitting. If you and a companion are on opposite ends of a sofa talking, a conversational space can be shaped and enhanced by the lighting.

You have to think in terms of the style and the finish and the aesthetic of the lighting fixtures that illuminate and adorn the passageways from one room to the other. You need light to go from here to there. The halls can have sconces or overhead lights. In the formal spaces, lighting is an important factor. I like to combine a center fixture in one room and lamplight in another room, so you get that shift in the movement of light that creates warmth and gives the space interest and vitality. So that there is no need of a passport, these elements have to have the same sensibility. You can't have a crystal chandelier in one room and a modern fixture in the other. Things have to connect stylistically, but they also have to differentiate themselves to avoid monotony and create a vivid sense that the house is alive. If you have a modern chandelier in the dining room, and there's a connecting hall, choose stainless steel or chrome fixtures for the hall.

The beauty of the house as a dwelling place is that you can borrow natural light from windows in every room. There is nothing better during the day than sunlight entering a room. Sunlight and natural light are the superlatives against which artificial light competes. But sunlight offers its own aesthetic. At night you can compensate for the lack of sunlight and differentiate day from night with table lamps and chandeliers. That's why crystal chandeliers are in dining rooms—they refract light around the room, fracturing it so that it glances off surfaces, enveloping the dining experience, setting it in its own space, bringing it brilliance and shimmer. That is why sconces are also used on dining room walls—to behave in the same way, elevating the act and ritual and art of eating by infusing it with the play of light.

BELOW
This coolly elegant bathroom is warmed by introducing the unexpected chair.

OPPOSITE
A classic white bath/dressing room gets a different look with a fanciful painted Victorian dresser.

6

INSIDE OUT

ARRIVAL

I always feel that arrival at a house is critical. It should have that quality of epiphany, that "aha!" moment—this is how it has to be. I know at a glance when I see a house that has this original look, that just-right quality that makes it unlike any other. Even though a house is a structure, it is not impersonal. What you see at the moment of arrival sets the tone and gives an idea of the artistic conception of the house. The image of the place where you live depends on first impressions. The shell is everything. It's your envelope. The exterior of the house relates to its style, and it forms the context for the building. Is the exterior made of shingles or clapboards? Is it natural and weathered or painted a color?

A stylish covered entrance greets guests, and the matching iron benches invite them to sit down for a moment of relaxation and enjoyment.

You usually arrive at a house in a car, not on foot. Simple things like placing a parking area at the back of the house avoid spoiling that first view of your handsome front facade, so that it is not blocked by cars. Your house is then part of its natural surround, with nothing man-made in the way.

EXTERIOR ARCHITECTURE

The architectural variables of the exterior affect the look of the house and form an accord with the way of life within. For the exterior, as for the interior, balance is important. There is nothing more unattractive than a lump of a house with no subtlety of shape. The balance of forms can make your house beautiful to look at when its parts are in the proper relation to each other. Then the house will have integrity and rhythm. For example, if someone doing a renovation wants a screened-in porch, it is important to decide on its placement in relation to the bulk of the house. The usual choice is to put it in the back, taking into account the views and the point of arrival. In my Remsenburg house, we reconfigured the outside, so that the living room and sunroom are on one end and the library is on the other, both with floor-to-ceiling windows. The middle section is the old saltbox. We made sure that it looked like an old house that grew, but that the proportion was still pleasant to the eye.

PREVIOUS SPREAD
This graceful curved arrival driveway sweeps toward the house, setting the tone of an opulent welcome.

LEFT
Mature plantings at the front of the house are a frame made of nature's abundance and unbeatable looks.

COLORS

Along with the architecture of the exterior and the landscape, the exterior colors strike the eye first. These colors are critical for the initial view of the house, and as a way to fit the house into its environment. They are an important liaison between the givens, the existing architectural and natural features, and the choices you make to leave your special stamp on the house.

In order to beautify the blend of architecture and landscape, the colors—of the house, the roof, the shutters, and the trim— must work in sync to capture the eye, the way makeup enhances a face to bring out its uniqueness, its glow. My experience with houses has schooled me in the subtleties and delights of exterior color. I like to wrap my head around the question of color— decorators are supposed to be on intimate terms with it—and I admit that it is one of my personal preferences. I gravitate naturally toward working with color, and I am often asked to help in decisions about the colors of the exterior. It is gratifying to draw the color spectrum of interior and exterior into a continuum, an orchestrated, synchronized whole. The choices offer excitement and variety, from paint on clapboard to shingles that can be stained or bleached. The shingle house might be gray with dark shutters or brown with cream-colored trim—chocolate to cream. Once I selected a terra-cotta color, once a pale yellow for a stucco house. If the house is made of a natural material—stone or wood— then the image of the exterior is nature's garb instead of painted lady. And I like to choose the colors of shutters and trim to go with the outfit, muted colors to give a veneer of venerability, perhaps, or brighter colors for greater whimsy and iconoclasm.

RIGHT
A classic Long Island shingle-style summerhouse.

OVERLEAF
The front entrance looking toward the back porch, with the dining room to the left and living room to the right.

TOP

The dining room with a door to the back terrace.
One of a pair of mirrors and sideboards.

ABOVE

A modern kitchen island for family coffee. The room
features cherry cabinetry with granite counters.

RIGHT

An ample dining table accommodates twelve people.
The flower painting is by Joseph Rafael.

PAGE 152

Many elements in this house are of materials reflecting
the abundant sunlight of its location. The glass hurricanes,
dessert and cheese domes, and lamp are examples. The
table surface also reflects and diffuses light.

PAGE 153

Light reflects off a dining table set for lunch.
A delicate lacework bamboo table rests proudly
in a bay window.

LEFT
The upstairs sitting area with an archway to the master suite. The watercolor is by Don Nice.

ABOVE
These Chinese storage steps, displaying a collection of boxes, create another light-catching opportunity. The three handcrafted wooden bowls on the coffee table continue the wood motif.

*Inside and out coexist
in this casual living room
with French doors to
the outside. Bamboo
and wicker chairs add
informality to soften
and enhance the room
style and to hint at the
outdoors. The paintings
are by Peter Plagens.*

LEFT

*Light reflects off a white
bookcase, one of a pair,
exhibiting a collection of
mocha ware and books.*

RIGHT

*The living room fireplace
wall looking toward
symmetrically placed
pine-paneled doors.*

Roof colors serve as a major announcement for the house, calling out to the viewer with a bold statement. There are slate roofs, dark and natural, and there are many commercial products, one better than the other, some plain, some all one color, some a mix of colors, and the prices are as varied as the materials. There are tin roofs and asbestos roofs in many colors, and there are copper roofs and terra-cotta roofs. Each of these can be arresting and beautiful as part of that first look. An example of an attractive house is a plain white farmhouse with a red roof that's fun: a red roof on a white farmhouse, from the American vernacular. There are natural clay roofs and glazed ones. I worked on a wonderful project on a private island in the Grenadines with a blue glazed tile roof and a pale lavender exterior, a true original.

BELOW
The Caribbean colors of this island property, with its pale lavender exterior and blue glazed ceramic tile roof, make it unique.

OPPOSITE
A white house with a porch and red roof is an American tradition.

LANDSCAPING

Landscape is important as backdrop, for harmony with the house. The usual beginning of landscaping is to level the ground, then put up the house, wasting the endowment. That's the easy way. In the process, most of the trees come down before anyone realizes that they have destroyed a valuable resource and a chance for beauty. It seems obvious, but isn't always, that if you buy property to build a house on, and the property has mature trees, you should figure out a way to save them—they give the umbrella to the house. A tree takes a hundred years to grow, one hundred years to live, and one hundred years to die. That's standard. If you start with a five-foot tree, you will wait a long time before it feels mature, so old landscaping is good. But it can look tired, which means that it has to be diminished and then embellished—diminished, but never removed. It would be a waste to destroy nature's bounty for a denuded piece of ground with a house and nothing around it.

One of the disciplines involved with the house is the landscape. Everyone forgets the landscaping budget, which has to be taken into consideration in the plans and in the deadlines for taking possession. If money is not an issue, you can get mature plantings and trees at a price. Perhaps you have an interest in gardening and know how to do things according to scale, so you can do some of it yourself. Often planting is confined to spring and fall, so you need a specific plan

BELOW
A living evergreen hedge replaces the expected fencing at courtside.

BOTTOM
A tree of epic proportions makes a magnificent umbrella for a nap in the hammock.

OPPOSITE TOP
Its partner is a Japanese maple, also red, gracing the other end of the pool.

OPPOSITE BOTTOM
A spectacular copper beech tree draws attention as it overhangs the pool area, offsetting nature's green with nature's red.

At the long end of the lap pool, walkways of local stone, hedges, and trees form a harmonious ensemble that seems to have occurred naturally.

*At the long end of the lap
pool, walkways of local
stone, hedges, and trees
form a harmonious*

LEFT
Alvar Aalto chairs make for easy lounging in this modern sunroom.

BELOW
This gracious outdoor dining area at the water's edge fits with the aesthetic of the house.

to make it work. Otherwise you live with nothing or with the possibility that it will be wrong, and the outside becomes a metaphoric thorn in your side. You need professional advice about embellishing the environment around the house. The plants you ordered may appear smaller than you had envisioned, and the landscape will seem to retreat into miniature, which means an unexpected and perhaps unwelcome wait for it to grow into mature beauty. Sometimes after the landscaping decisions have been made, problems arise—people are busy or it's the wrong season or you can't get the plants on time. Suddenly you are moving in when the outside is a mud hole with planting going on. What about your beautiful white sofas?

The entire front of the house is
windowed to take advantage
of the water views. The room
showcases Gae Aulenti chairs
and marble tables.

LEFT

A stone fireplace in this Connecticut house adds texture to the living room space.

ABOVE

Large windows are left undraped for an uninterrupted view of the garden.

OVERLEAF

The upstairs hall and gallery.

Because the visual arts are partners, people often ask me to review the master plan designed by the landscape people. If I am involved with outside areas—patios, porches, eating pavilions, exterior spaces, screened-in porches—I feel it is important to attend to the immediate environ of that space, just as a painter will attend to the background of a painting. Then there will be continuity between in and out.

The geographic position of the house, as well as whether the house is informal or formal, will determine the landscape style. You might have an interest in studying plant material and giving the landscape your personal touch rather than just letting it happen arbitrarily.

The landscaping and its colors should blend with the rest of the house, although they are not necessarily matching outfits. You may want to educate yourself about flowering or blooming plants, or you may be happier with evergreens. Perhaps you will elect to have trees that change color in the fall, like the Japanese maple, for bursts of momentary brilliance. I might suggest blue hydrangeas to smooth the way if the furniture inside is in soft neutrals. There are certain color schemes that should not be violated. If the interior isn't multicolored, then you shouldn't have multicolored flowers outside. You should allocate them to a cutting garden that is off on its own and perhaps concentrate on white flowers to avoid discordant notes. Or if there are pink peonies, perhaps they should have their place in the sun by the pool or tennis court, as their own element of the landscape language. H. F. DuPont, founder of Winterthur, now a museum in Delaware, was a definitive style maker. He had the gardeners plant flowers to match the interiors of the rooms—he particularly favored the colors red and fuchsia. Every season they changed the flowers and the slipcovers to match.

PORCHES AND OUTDOOR SPACES

The porches of my childhood are such a vivid memory that I rejoice in designing them and other outdoor spaces, and I consider them, although in the amenity category, almost a necessity. Porches give a sense of well-being, of comfort and community and family togetherness, and of the transition between indoors and out, forming part of both aspects of the domestic environment. The memories from my past that influence my life now would not be the same without its porches. If porches could talk, they would probably tell enough stories to fill libraries, unraveling an epic of America and its lives. Porches are certainly part of our collective consciousness and of our popular culture, with or without rocking chairs. They provide graciousness as well as folksiness in the outside environment and an inviting spot to sit

BELOW
A lattice porch enclosure filters the heat and protects against strong sunlight.

BOTTOM
Porches are comfortable outdoor rooms, places for casual gatherings.

OPPOSITE
The color blue acts as a visual reference between indoors and out.

down and chat, dream, reflect, sing, or look at the moon. It would be a shame to have a house without a space that leads from landscape to interior, a passage to a different zone. A house without a porch has a disconnect between out and in—it is too abrupt. Human beings were made to live outside as well as in interior spaces. Porches ease this flow.

Porches vary in their character and functions. There are sun porches, front porches, screened porches, open and covered porches. And porches are only one of several al fresco living spaces that add to the variety of life. I am often asked to plan furniture for outdoor spaces, which may include patios or porches, a fenced or hedged pool, an outside garden, or a little tennis pavilion adjacent to the tennis court. We see these areas as integral parts of the house. To furnish them, we might place a glider or a swing or sofas with comfortable upholstered cushions that make it inviting to sit outdoors. An appealing bench or a hammock might also go under your favorite tree, an ornament for the landscape. We are fortunate now to have newly invented outdoor fabrics that do not absorb moisture like the fabrics of the past, so more color and interest in the outdoor furniture and cushions is possible.

LEFT
Today, outdoor furniture is designed to repel moisture. There is great variety in pattern, shape, and color available in both furnishings and upholstery. Here is an example of how visual appeal can add to a sheltered al fresco area.

RIGHT TOP
Folding chairs and a table are used here for more flexibility on a screened porch.

RIGHT BOTTOM
A covered porch with painted wicker furniture.

With or without walls, the spaces of the house and its precinct
should be in open communication. The dialogue between indoors
and out should observe the dictates of balance and harmony.
The outdoor and indoor spaces should be compatible—I see
compatibility in everything. When you arrive at the house, you
hope to see an environment integrated in scale to the house
and to the interior furnishings, so that the overall impression is
unified. And when you look out the windows from inside, you
don't want a shock when you see something that bears no
relevance to the room you are in. You want the fluidity we all need
between nature and nurture, between landscape and living space.

PREVIOUS SPREAD
*The pool of a beautifully
modern Florida house is
seamlessly integrated into
the architecture.*

ABOVE AND RIGHT
*Simple sofas and club chairs
by Charles Pfister help
exaggerate the architectural
angles.*

FAR LEFT
This guest room features the client's collection of American Spongeware.

LEFT
Step down to the library/media room. Classic Mies van der Rohe leather daybed at left. Hans Wegner chairs are comfortable, yet do not encumber the space.

BELOW
The master bedroom overlooks the water, the focus of a neutral, peaceful space.

7

AMENITIES

In designing your house, you can make provisions for features that have particular importance to you and your family. These are the amenities, added elements that are not strictly necessary. The word *amenity* comes from the Latin word for *pleasant,* so amenities in a house are for the pleasures that life can afford. They are for special interests, indulgences, entertainment, extras, even frills. Think of them as accessorizing the house. They range from simple pleasures to true luxuries, touches that go beyond required living spaces. Amenities come in various guises, from the more common family room or porch to the rarer and more luxurious massage room or home theater. Amenities may be recreational or health related, or they may be spaces such as family rooms, libraries, or patios, for various domestic experiences. Perhaps the library exemplifies the

Who wouldn't want to nestle into the armchairs of this library,
to read or chat against the backdrop of bookshelves and fireplace and
oversize window looking at the garden?

most versatile and gracious of amenities, in the range of its uses and in its ability to be a hideaway for quiet moments and a change of scene for social gatherings.

In some cases, the amenities can become as important to the dwellers as the necessities. I work to integrate these specialized personal choices and desires so that they fit the overall concept of the house. The house is for you to live in as you choose—the American dream, with your individual dreams included.

Libraries—We love libraries, even if we are not bibliophiles or scholars. I love my books, and I feel that books are universally appreciated as documents containing worlds of wonder and ideas and stories, and as objects beloved in their look, their feel, their uses and enjoyments. I have a library in Remsenburg full of all my favorite books, the books I have been collecting since I began to buy them for my children. I always loved children's books, and now my library is so full that I need another library.

This room was standard issue in older homes. The very word *library* conjures up another era, when people read as a purposeful activity, as a pleasure and as entertainment and as a way to engage with the world. Libraries started as rooms for those who wanted to be informed or who loved books and the joy of reading or referencing favorite topics. But what of the library today? What of its many incarnations? Is the library reserved for the socially and financially upscale, a special-interest book-lined niche in the design cosmos? Is it a room that just looks nice, rather than a space where what you do matters? The library is a place where books are featured, a throwback to the time before the library gave way to the office. But what a luxury and gift to the family if you reinstate the concept, then update it for modern times.

You can reinvigorate the idea of a library, give new life to that hallowed, venerated space, with its universal aesthetic of books, by blending past and present. You can design the library in a number of ways to underline its potential for social interchange and for separation from the crowd. I want to express the many faces of the

library as I adapt it to the modern world. I recognize that books in themselves occupy a unique place in the design firmament. There is something in all of us that loves a wall of books. We feel good when they surround us, when we sit in front of the multicolored backdrop of spines. The book is a fabulous invention—a deceptively simple technology we take for granted and overlook, housing for the world of words and ideas. Unlike our obsession-producing computer, with its neon flash, books are appealing visually, as well as meaningful and practical. We like to be in their company, even when they are on the shelf. They cast a benevolent glow around a room, providing us with the ideal, homey atmosphere, the surround for warm lamplight. The bookcase as design feature is a wonderful quick fix, a shortcut to a great look, unparalleled in the creation of coziness and domestic well-being. I like to take advantage of the physical and visual appeal of the library as an environment, as it plays a role in various aspects of our lives.

The library can be a social space or a private one. Traditionally a haven for booklovers, the library is a retreat for moments of solitude and contemplation. You can design it as a proper library, with lighting to read by and your favorite subject matter, and it can be as classical as a traditional library, with books in categories. Historically, a library had a library table, but now there are comfortable chairs, a sofa, and good lights and perhaps a desk, all of which expand the possibilities for this versatile room in the life of the house. Today, the library, designed for varied uses, can be an inviting setting for part of a dinner party, for cocktails or an after-dinner drink. It might even serve as an occasional den for male bonding, with or without cigars.

TOP
My library has my favorite books, which I have collected over time. Adjustable shelves accommodate larger book sizes in loosely arranged subject groupings.

ABOVE
An Italian bookcase and matching paneling create an evening retreat.

OPPOSITE
This library features the owner's collection of birdhouses.

The library is part of all the divisions of space in the house, social-formal, casual-family, and private. It can be a crossroads or a quiet spot for the life of the mind, or it can provide an opportunity for spatial exploration at that moment in a gathering when a journey to another space is the right thing.

Study/Home Offices—Libraries can double as studies. The library-study has become a multipurpose room with overlapping functions—for work or for reference or for simple enjoyment, solitary or otherwise. In a large-scale house, you might have an upstairs study for calls and letters. Years ago it used to be called the morning room—in the 1800s women would write their correspondence there. Furnish a study according to its use. If it's for occasional use, for weekend paperwork, you would want comfortable furniture with a work surface and computer access, a TV and sofa for sports or an afternoon nap. It needs electrical outlets for printers, faxes, and answering machine, plus file, book, and supply storage—and a window with a view.

Family Rooms—Family rooms are on the simpler, less extravagant end of the spectrum of amenities. They are fairly common today, and you do not need a luxurious house to have one. This modern "recreation" room is usually near the kitchen. If I am planning a family room, I love to include old-fashioned tactile things, as well as game boards and a place for school projects and for a snack. I also feel that toy storage is essential, and it teaches as well as occupies. This room is not just a TV room, but a television, especially larger scale, should be accommodated, whether it is hidden or exposed.

The playroom is related to the family room, but it is a separate interior space for children's play. It often has overscaled features such as slides and climbing frames, and it might be the place for moving vehicles and educational toys. The safety factor is important—these rooms allow parents to monitor children's play.

BELOW
A comfortable game room on the second floor of a country guesthouse.

OPPOSITE
The ultimate screening room.

Media Rooms—The media room is attaining the status of a
given in new houses. It runs the gamut from lesser to greater
dimensions, from a space for a large-screen TV, which often needs
a room of its own, to a minitheater with movie screen and seating
and sound. Now that movies are making their way out of theaters
and are more available at home than ever before, people are
constructing spaces for movie watching in their homes. In rural
communities, where movie theaters are not as accessible, people
are putting in media rooms, particularly in second homes, so they
can keep their family together for recreation at night.

Exercise and Massage and Dressing Rooms—Also in the amenity category are the rooms geared to adult recreational activities. In our health-conscious twenty-first century, most houses of a certain status make provision for a room for exercise. This might be a simple space with a TV and treadmill or a more elaborate room furnished with workout machines and a whirlpool. The exercise room for yoga enthusiasts might be in a carpeted basement. If you have a leftover space off the exercise room, and if you adhere to the ritual of massage, you might want a massage room. The oils and other paraphernalia, including special towels that don't go in the everyday laundry, can be allocated to that space. The room can even take on a certain elegance, with attractive bottles for oils and neat stacks of towels. After you've used your muscles, a massage relaxes, and for added benefit, you might put a sauna off the exercise room. These modern amenities are decidedly in the luxury category, but in some parts of the world saunas are found in most houses, even modest ones.

A more traditional but no less luxurious feature, also geared to your personal care, is the dressing room, which relocates this daily necessity from the end of the bed or the bathroom. In Irish or English houses in the eighteenth century, old-fashioned cupboards called clothes presses existed in place of closets, but in today's world we can create built-in cupboards and make the space roomy enough to be a dressing room. This luxury can be yours, or possibly his and hers. With a few adjustments, you can design it for collective use.

Guest Rooms—Guest rooms are common amenities, not quite in the category of luxury, but beyond necessity. The key is to make the guest room welcoming to your guest, with quality bedding and a good reading light and carpet. I prefer fresh white for linens, and down pillows (add two firmer ones in a closet for an alternative)—they radiate comfort and luxury. Choose a tweed or small-scale pattern for an area rug on a wood floor—it's more inviting than a boring solid color. And opt for practical bedside tables—leave that rickety Victorian heirloom in the basement. Good reading lamps can be inexpensive but sturdy and attractive in design. And it would be nice for the guest to have a reading chair to go with the lamp. Make sure guests have everything they need and are not embarrassed by having to ask for something. I stay in many of the guest rooms that I do, and I like to notice what's missing—did I forget something? We provide a luggage rack and small flashlights if the lights go out. We include everything in these guest rooms to make a guest feel at home, to confer well-being, to beckon. Think of a hotel room. And remember, just as in a hotel, it's nice to have a view.

LEFT
Shutters are used as windows in this bedroom in the tropics.

TOP RIGHT
Anyone would want to be a guest in a guest room with this eighteenth-century Spanish bed, carefully enlarged and restored.

BOTTOM RIGHT
A painting of flowers on the wall, a flower-patterned quilt in matching colors, and a porch off this master bedroom serve as a lovely comment on the closeness of nature outside the window.

OPPOSITE
Breakfast at the kitchen island.

BELOW
The piano alcove gets a special blessing from the window and its glowing reflection in the ebonized piano.

OVERLEAF
Tack room furniture was added to humanize the experience, with the original stone walls and floors and wooden ceiling beams.

Breakfast Rooms—The breakfast room has become our modern-day nesting place. It's like a hug. You want to make sure the children can flop down there on their way to school or join you when you are cooking or when you take time off to sit down. I try for brightness and a feeling of relaxation and warmth, with a mix of the color of the walls and the choice of materials for tables and benches, as well as their placement. I like to make the breakfast room a cheery place. I also recommend lots of windows. Family space near the kitchen is a good place for intimate details and for collections of things that go with the style of the kitchen—your antique bowls or hammered-silver platters.

The breakfast room has replaced the dining room for family dinners, so that the dining room's job has become entertaining, hospitality, and special-occasion dining. Try using this occasional-use room for informal or formal buffets. It's a perfect opportunity to utilize an elegant, attractive space, adding to its function as the place for family activities.

Other Amenities—There are other smaller or less orthodox amenities—an alcove for a grand piano, for example. In a house in Ireland that is also about the grounds and the horses, there is a tack room. And in some houses there are mudrooms for coming in from outside—it's always good to have an entrance with a stone floor to accommodate inclement weather.

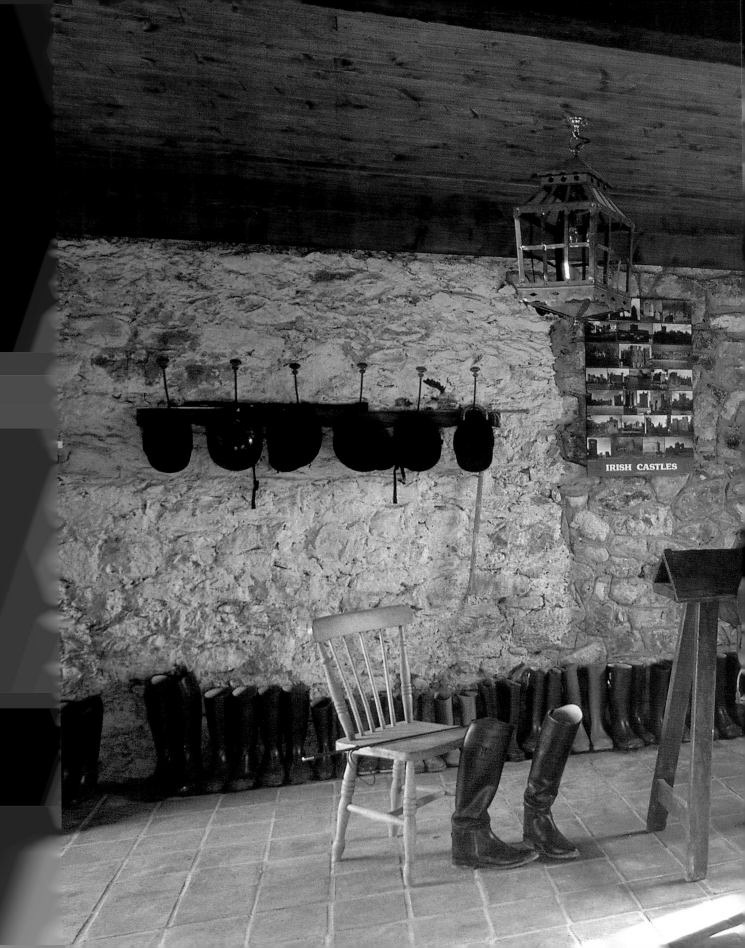

IRISH CASTLES

- *Now you are ready* to ask, what does it mean to have a house, whether you build it, renovate it, or move into a ready-to-go? You may not have any idea of what it takes, and so you haven't thought of this crucial preliminary, the plan that makes it all work, the simple step-by-step approach that can fit everyone's circumstances. If you follow this process, you will avoid the pitfalls of being overwhelmed, which is the state of mind that many people new to houses fall into. Tailor the plan to your budget so that a logistical nightmare does not ensue. Now is the time to use your list-making and organizational skills.

- *The plan is a system* of reminders, an agenda, a to-do list. It avoids nasty surprises, things that get lost in translation between idea and execution. The beginning, when you first look at the house or at the plans of the house, is the time to provide for your needs and desires. This kind of organization and anticipation of circumstances can save you a lot of hand-wringing later. It is a way to simplify, to have a relaxing and positive approach, avoiding the agonies and expense of after-the-fact patches.

- *Your personal plan* of attack will vary with your personal style. Ask yourself, Am I going to spend a day or a week on this? Will I check out builders in the area? Am I going to be a perfectionist, or just get an overview? If your budget is limited, start cautiously, and make the right choices. The money you spend in bringing in a builder or architect to help you, whether it involves the cost of the service or the personality of the person, is your smart money, your best investment.

- *Building a house* is a major undertaking, and it's for the hardy. The drawn-out process of drawing and designing and estimating may not be compatible with your habits. That newly built palace of yours usually takes one or two years, but I've worked on houses that took four years to build, depending on size and on construction conditions in a certain area. It's good to consider this wide range of possibilities in advance. It may be winter and there will be no chance of pouring the foundation until spring. Building from scratch, though, will allow for the exact nuances you want, in all their specificity—his and hers bathrooms, special closet requirements, a large eat-in kitchen. Formal dining room for twelve? If you have books, make sure you have bookcases or a library. It may seem that this is belaboring the obvious, but in my experience, people can overlook what seems self-evident unless it is staring them in the face or until they have forgotten something and realize they have made a mistake. A careful plan eliminates these missteps.

- *Renovating a house* is a less lengthy affair, and its built-in shortcuts make it appealing to those less inclined to throw a considerable portion of their lives and energy into building from the ground up. Renovating gives you something to grab on to and experience firsthand, so you are not facing a blank slate. Even then it's hard for the average person to envision chopping off half of the room, although it can be done. As a layperson, you may have difficulty reading building plans. They are hard to visualize until you have a picture before your eyes—until the structure is in place, the walls are up, and you can take a walk through and experience the space. Then, is there a problem with the size or location of a room? If you acknowledge that something is amiss—a window is not as it should be, for example—a small shift can often improve things significantly, and better sooner than later. If you inherit the nuances of the former owner, whether it is recessed lighting in the ceiling or a kitchen that should be replaced, you can change it before it's too late.

■ *You may prefer* a house that is ready to go, built, painted, and appointed and in place. Maybe you've seen a picture postcard and have always loved that Cape Cod, or there's a house on a hill, or near the water, or in a particular style that you like. In this case, all you have to think about is furnishing and decorating and covering windows and floors, giving the house a face-lift.

Whether you are building or renovating, I always recommend working with the builder and visiting the site to get hands-on feedback. Get a carpenter or a local builder in to improve things, not just the kitchen or bathrooms—anything that doesn't work. When the paint is on the walls and the furniture has been upholstered, it's late for that kind of editing. These simple steps can avoid dismaying loopholes and lead to an outcome you choose yourself.

For a luxury property, it is not uncommon to have an architect, a designer, and a landscape architect to work with the builder, not just through the design phase but also through the entire building process. If you don't have that multifaceted expertise, a committee of the whole, to give you the best available knowledge culled from years of experience, you will be burdened with the necessity of attending to details you probably are not equipped to deal with. You will not be able to take advantage of the education and eye and experience of experts to smooth your passage to your goals.

MOVING

Once everything is complete, including cabinetry and lighting fixtures, you are faced with the staggering project of moving. Make it easier by planning for that, too. Otherwise the act of moving into a new house becomes all consuming, a descent into chaos.

- *Take an appraising* look at your possessions. If you are going to reuse things, arrange them in your mind's eye. Do you want a new look, a reshuffle to animate a tired furniture group?

- *If you have pieces* of furniture, a bed or sofa or cabinet or coffee table, allocate them to another space: put the sofa in the family room, then buy a new sofa for the living room, so that everything feels original and offers a changed view. This will allow you to select new acquisitions for more major rooms, and it will invigorate you and add dynamism to the life of your possessions and of the house. Everyone needs a new look periodically, a spark of renewal. Houses are like people—that new ensemble can lift up your whole appearance.

- *If the carpets* are down and fiber sealed and the curtains and shades are hung, you can pack things appropriately by room, and the orderliness will give you a sense that all is right with the world.

- *You can pack* your most private of possessions—the family silver or a collection of pillboxes—in one box if you are afraid they might get lost, then carry the box over by hand.

You can send books over for the library, so that they can be dusted and put into place.

These simple steps in the planning process can make the difference between order and chaos during the actual move.

DIVIDE AND CONQUER:
MAKE A BUDGET FOR EACH ROOM

You may never have thought about a budget before starting your house project. You may have wanted to live in a particular neighborhood, where the houses cost a certain amount, but you have not thought about the budget for decorating the house. You need to be conscious of costs so that they do not jump out at you unannounced. Once you've done the landscaping, bought the kitchen cabinets, and paid the closing costs, it's no good to realize you can't afford to buy furniture. A house has a big budget, sensible or extravagant, including all the professional fees, the cost of the contractor, the furniture, window coverings, flooring, kitchen cabinets, and material for the bathrooms. In my office we always start with the budget. It's a bit like taming an elephant, but it has to be done.

Divide and conquer is important. I always recommend a budget for every room.

- *When people move* into a house, there is an order to their interest in rooms: the living room is always first, the master bedroom is next. The living room is most important because it forms the first impression for visitors to your home. It is the stage of your success and of social and financial status, your face to the world. You can give rein to your imagination and creativity here.

- *The dining room* takes less application—it's a dining table and chairs and a server, a more functional space. It almost designs itself.

- *The master bedroom* is about comfort, the place you as owners have worked so hard to enjoy.

- *There are necessities* in a house, and you must be practical and realistic. Kitchens and bathrooms are essential—you have to cook meals and you need bathrooms that work.

I feel that completing a room becomes an enjoyment on its own. If you walk through a room that has no curtains and bare floors, it feels unfinished and you feel uneasy, as if you are trespassing in a place that is still in process. A sense of completion makes for contentment.

- *If the living room* and master bedroom are important, finish them. Don't just put in a bed with an old bedspread and buy a couple of chairs, so that the room looks slapdash.

- *If your plan* of attack is to complete all the rooms, use your wiles and your powers of self-persuasion to invent a way to keep it within the budget. It may mean taking a different angle of vision—instead of having everything radiate spanking newness, reusing the children's beds or buying furniture on sale and combining it in a stylish way can result in an interesting ensemble you just realized can work without a disastrous depletion of your funds.

My theory is that you will be more comfortable within the skin of the house if you complete the parts you decide to do first. Houses are not all in the present. They do have futures.

A postscript to budget concerns: if you are thinking in terms of practicality and budget, make sure to allow one extravagance, to make decorating feel special and to give yourself a personal pat on the back for all your effort—a chef's oven, 600-thread-count cotton sheets, a blanket chest you thought was too expensive, or luxuriant raw-silk upholstery. It will give your house a unique profile, and it will be an exhilarating final flourish to a job well done.

ONE-OF-A-KIND HOUSE

Houses can spring from the imagination into full-blown creations, works of art, reaching their zenith in the one-of-a-kind house, a house the creator conceives from the ground up into something that has never been seen or built before. The one-of-a-kind house is not modeled according to a style that informs other houses, nor is it a "kind" of house made of common building blocks.

The one-of-a-kind house can begin with an idea, a circumstance, a natural feature, or a purpose served in the life of a person. Often the locale is the incentive for this kind of distinctive dwelling. When I design a one-of-a-kind house, I consider the elements of the locale that integrate into its language. It is important to design the house to feel indigenous to the region in which it is located, as well as to the local architecture. If the locale is the imperative for the

Actual trees support and adorn a living room space.

house, it can give it a novel, unprecedented aspect, which is exemplified in various one-of-a-kind houses I have worked on.

One of these houses is a Southwestern ranch on a Colorado property with a river running through it. In keeping with the character of life on the mountain range, the color, culture, and flavor of the ranch as a facility for both work and play speak the particular visual language of the locale. The modern-built structure should, if only in a decorative way, suggest earlier times. With stone fireplaces, exposed wood construction, and rustic furnishings, and the rich textures and colors used in area carpets and throughout the house, the peacefulness of this lifestyle choice is articulated in a distinctive ranch-style structure.

PREVIOUS SPREAD
A Colorado ranch house.

ABOVE
*The authentic one-story ranch
sits at river's edge.*

OPPOSITE
*A high-ceilinged living room features
a stone fireplace with a pair of
decorative copper inserts. The brick-
red upholstery goes well with the
wood construction and affords
comfortable seating. Wild West
elements give punch to the room—
antlers adorn the mantel, and a set
of horses, coaches, and wagons in
miniature decorates a wooden table.*

TOP

A stand of recently planted trees on a knoll at the approach to this ranch property looks as if it has always been part of the landscape.

ABOVE

Contrasting piping defines this chair of saddle-colored leather.

RIGHT

A red and tan Southwestern carpet grounds the furniture in this airy room. Materials of the region were used throughout the house. Here they include a pair of leather-upholstered chairs and decorative pieces suggestive of the locale. Small wooden boxes, a bark canoe, and small sculptures of a bighorn sheep and a horse sit on the tables.

OPPOSITE
The guest hall looking toward the stone fireplace in the sitting room.

TOP
The colors, shapes, and textures of this master bedroom combine to elevate it into a work of art. The wood wall, punctured with four square recesses, frames and throws into relief the curving leather headboard and the collection of antique pillows of variegated materials and patterns splashed with gold. The specific mix of surfaces, textures, and forms results in visually arresting, balanced and dynamic proportions and rhythms, creating a striking, almost musical harmony and beauty.

CENTER
In the master bath, Shaker-style vanities are offset by a pair of antique mirrors.

BOTTOM
The children's guest bedroom showcases matching beds with cowboy quilts, cowboy lamp, and gingham shams.

This organically designed and developed lodge is built from the wood of an aging cherry orchard on the site. Seeded wildflowers are in the foreground.

OPPOSITE
Flanked by Pugin cast-iron firedogs, this monumental stone fireplace is central to a guest reading room. Tree branches arch overhead, sheltering the space and creating a romantic fantasy room.

BELOW LEFT
Actual logs are used as a fireplace surround, reminiscent of bonfires in the open.

BELOW RIGHT
An ornamental iron fire screen in front of the stone fireplace, with the brown and green tones of the comfortable seating, invites guests.

Another unusual house, an eccentric lodge, derives from a feature of the landscape, an accident of nature that inspired the owner and architect. Using as raw material an aging orchard of cherry trees on the verge of extinction, they milled the trees to build the house, a reincarnation of the cherry orchard. Set in a field of wildflowers, with stone and glass walls overlooking the mountains, the house springs directly from nature and its rhythms. The furnishings are handmade by artisans to go with the structure, and we had the carpets bordered by white birch trees. The materials are organic. The cherry trees in evidence on floors and walls breathe life into the dwelling. We did the children's rooms in old milk paint. In Early America, pigment was mixed with milk, then allowed to sour before being used as paint. It doesn't cover as well as today's paint, but it does lend a distinctive old-time finish. And so this house of nature has a folktale aspect, a true house in, or of, the woods.

OPPOSITE
*Guest cabin curtains
and carpet are kept light.
Furnishings are richly
colored to balance the
rustic walls and ceiling.*

RIGHT
*One wall in the living
room is made entirely of
glass to take advantage
of the western view
overlooking a mountain
range, showcasing
weather, sky, and sunsets.*

OVERLEAF LEFT
*A cigar-store Indian and
companion bear watch
over the porch.*

OVERLEAF RIGHT
*One of many corners,
this one with richly
textured finishes and
folk art comes together
harmoniously.*

An extraordinary house, the vision of the owners, is a formal, historically classic American house. It is a masterpiece of architectural detailing. The wraparound porch (seen on page 237) is not only beautifully symmetrical but also affords the opportunity to capture views on all sides of the building. Natural gaslight adjacent to traditional dark green shutters at the front door replaces electrified side lanterns. With its reference to a classic, historic style, this house sits proudly on its waterside site, a brilliant blend of architecture, nature, and design.

LEFT
Greek Revival-style architecture.

RIGHT
The three-story center hall ends in a clerestory dome.

PAGE 237
Who could imagine anything more magical than this evening view, with the moon shedding its glow on the water and on the classically designed house?

These houses are rare creations, and

they deserve celebration on their own. Each one

is as individual as a person in all his or her

quirky uniqueness. Coming from particular

temperaments and tastes, they are affirmations

of originality, singular inspirations,

like other works of art.

EPILOGUE

YOUR PERFECT PACKAGE

Houses are a fundamental human phenomenon. They fill a need. They reflect ideas about how people live. The houses in this book are meant as inspirations to illuminate the world of possibility that opens when you choose your own house, with all of its ingredients and variations. They provide an entrée and a different perspective for you, the home buyer, as you discover ways of giving your house its own unique character. The overriding purpose of the book is to illustrate the best way to acknowledge and execute your various needs to create the best house for you. All the elements of your house form the package that is the whole house. Why not have your perfect package?

Each house speaks its own language. Each house has its own animating spirit. The building may be colonial or modern, brick or shingle, but the notion of the spirit of a house applies to all styles and kinds of houses. The houses in this book are in diverse styles, but they are consistent in their flow. They are in harmony with the peripheral structure, the architectural shell. The furnishings, the interior design, and the use of spaces exhibit stylistic continuity from start to finish, although this does not necessitate using the same style throughout. But the structure is not just a physical object. It is the spirit that draws the house together. It unifies the house.

You are the arbiter of what to include architecturally, stylistically, and aesthetically as you invest the house with your spirit. With the knowledge imparted here, you will be equipped with expanded ideas of design and with the tools to create your own home. You might pay attention to a staircase you had not considered or realize that hanging pictures is relevant to how a room will look. You can think about how you want one room to look with another room, and you can appreciate how a certain style will fit with where you live. You can open your mind and challenge your imagination.

I've offered my reflections here on what houses are and what they mean, as well as my designer know-how and my approach to helping you understand what to anticipate when you fall in love with a house. Achieving the look of home, creating welcoming places for living, places that last and are not empty or ephemeral style setters are accomplishments that require thought and creativity and investment of self. My object is to share my insights and artistry from my years in design, whatever the style or location of the house, to help you to find ways to use your own experience to create your home. By considering these houses and following the ideas and examples in the book, you can devise a formula of your own.

And then perhaps you will take something away from this book that you did not bring to it and use that to create a beloved and artistic dwelling that will be better for your having seen and read about houses here.

The result will be your perfect package.

PAGE 238
The large windows provide the perfect place to display the owner's mercury glass collection, which sparkles in the sunlight. With the mountains and the pool beyond, this small arrangement blends natural setting, architecture, interior design, beautiful furniture, treasured objects, and light.

RIGHT
The view of the mountain range is the focus of this room. The windows are left undraped to enhance it. The furniture, upholstered in white, was chosen purposely not to compete with the view.

ACKNOWLEDGMENTS

Building a house involves several people: architects, contractors, and landscapers, to name a few. Writing a book requires a comparable group effort. First and foremost I would like to thank Sally Steinberg. Her patience and insight in modifying my thoughts and concepts shaped fluid text that is not only beautifully written, but also very informative. Thank you to everyone at HarperCollins, especially Cassie Jones, for her enthusiasm for a follow-up to *Rooms*, and for her precise editing talent, guidance, and advice. To Joel Avirom, for his attention to detail and artistry in creating what is an elegant and stunning finished product. My deep appreciation to Pam Bernstein, an encouraging colleague and friend.

Thanks to everyone at Gomez Associates for all the hard work that transformed each project into a spectacular house. I would especially like to thank Mary Dobbin, Karen Laurence, and Renee Infantino. Their collective efforts helped organize the book while making the process enjoyable and effortless. Many thanks to Carolyn Gregg for her sensitive floral artistry present in many of the photographs. Thank you to all my clients for inviting us into their homes and allowing us to celebrate and share elements of design. To all the architects and photographers with whom I have had the pleasure to collaborate; they are my inspiration and I appreciate all the things they have taught me over the years. A special thanks to Paige Rense, a champion of beautiful design and a generous and supportive friend.

Last, I want to thank my family and friends for helping make my house a home. One can have all the right pillows, flowers, and furniture, but without the people you love, a house is just a house.